Clinical Laboratory Law Answer Book

AF691895

Christina W. Fleps, JD
Partner
O'Connor & Hannan
Washington, DC

An Aspen Publication®
Aspen Publishers, Inc.
Gaithersburg, Maryland
1994

This publication is designed to provide accurate and authoritative information in regard to the Subject Matter covered. It is sold with the understanding that the publisher is not engaged in rendering legal, accounting, or other professional service. If legal advice or other expert assistance is required, the service of a competent professional person should be sought. *(From a Declaration of Principles jointly adopted by a Committee of the American Bar Association and a Committee of Publishers and Associations.)*

Library of Congress Cataloging-in-Publication Data
Fleps, Christina W.
Clinical laboratory law answer book/Christina W. Fleps
p. cm.
Includes bibliographical references and index.
ISBN 0-8342-0530-0
1. Pathological laboratories–Law and legislation–United States. I. Title.
[DNLM: QY 33 AA1 FSc 1994]
KF3826.L3F8 1994
344. 73'03212–DC20
[347.3043212]
DNLM/DLC
For Library of Congress
94-11811
CIP

Copyright © 1994 by Aspen Publishers, Inc.
All rights reserved.

Aspen Publishers, Inc., grants permission for photocopying for personal or internal use. This consent does not extend to other kinds of copying, such as copying for general distribution, for advertising or promotional purposes, for creating new collective works, or for resale. For information, address Aspen Publishers, Inc., Permissions Department, 200 Orchard Ridge Drive, Gaithersburg, Maryland 20878.

Editorial Resources: Ruth Bloom

Library of Congress Catalog Card Number: 94-11811
ISBN: 0-8342–0530-0

Printed in the United States of America

1 2 3 4 5

Table of Contents

List of Questions

1—Federal Laboratory Certification under CLIA '88

2

Medicare Reimbursement for Clinical Laboratory Tests

3

State Licensure of Clinical Laboratories

4

Fraud and Abuse

5

Clinical Laboratory Billing

6

Clinical Laboratory Advertising

7

Medicaid Overview

8

Blood Banks

9

AIDS and the Laboratory

10

Drug Testing

11

The Laboratory As Employer

12

Malpractice

Introduction

The *Clinical Laboratory Law Answer Book* is designed for clinical laboratory managers, employees, and investors who need quick and authoritative answers on a broad spectrum of questions concerning legal and regulatory requirements affecting clinical laboratory operations. The *Answer Book* addresses the laboratory in its role as a provider of testing services, as a billing entity, as a business engaging in advertising and promotional activities, as an employer, and as a provider of specialized services such as drug testing and blood banking. The *Answer Book* addresses laws and regulations both at the federal and state levels.

This guide is intended to provide a ready reference and a comprehensive overview on issues about which laboratory managers, employees, and investors must be knowledgeable. It is intended to familiarize everyone involved in the management and operation of the laboratory with requirements that the facility must meet and with the sanctions and penalties that may occur if applicable requirements are not satisfied.

The *Answer Book* does not attempt to address this broad array of issues in great detail, but rather to give the clinical laboratory professional a working knowledge of the entire range of standards and requirements affecting a clinical laboratory. For more in-depth knowledge about these matters, the laboratory professional is advised to consult references identified in the text, and in particular, the *Laboratory Regulation Manual (LRM)*, a comprehensive, four-volume work that deals with clinical laboratory requirements in more exhaustive detail. The LRM was originally written in 1976 by Hope S. Foster and H. Robert Halper, both partners in the Washington, D.C., law firm of O'Connor & Hannon. Subsequently, the LRM has been updated quarterly by contributing editors working under the direction of Foster and Halper until Mr. Halper's death in 1988, then under the direction of Ms. Foster.

This *Answer Book* could not have been written without substantial reliance on the LRM. The author wishes to express her sincere appreciation to Ms. Foster and the various contributing editors who have updated the LRM under her direction since 1976.

How To Use This Book

This *Answer Book* attempts to use simple language and avoid complex terminology when possible, although technical language that is necessary and appropriate to descriptions of laboratory operations appears at various points in the book.

CITATIONS

Citations of authority are provided as research aids for those who need to pursue particular items in greater detail.

QUESTION NUMBERING

The question numbering system is simple, numbering questions consecutively within each chapter.

QUESTION LISTS

The List of Questions following the Table of Contents is a detailed listing of questions intended to help the reader locate areas of immediate interest. The Table of Contents at the beginning of the volume identifies the page on which each list of questions appears.

INDEX

At the back of the book is an index, provided as a further aid to locating specific information. All references in the index are to question numbers rather than page numbers.

ABBREVIATIONS

Due to the breadth of the subject area, various terms are either abbreviated or designated by acronyms throughout the book. Generally, the first time each such abbreviation is used, it follows the full term with which it is associated in the text.

1

Federal Laboratory Certification under CLIA '88

Q.1:1 What is CLIA'88?

CLIA'88 (Clinical Laboratory Improvement Amendments of 1988), 42 U.S.C. §263a, is a federal law that subjects virtually all clinical laboratories operating in the United States to comprehensive federal quality regulation. CLIA'88 replaces the Clinical Laboratory Improvement Act of 1967 (CLIA'67), which regulated only those laboratories operating interstate.

Q.1:2 What major events led to the enactment of CLIA'88?

A long succession of media exposés and congressional hearings concerning quality problems in clinical laboratory testing in 1987 and 1988 preceded the enactment of CLIA'88. These events began on February 2 and 3, 1987, when the *Wall Street Journal* published Walt Bogdanich's eventually Pulitzer-prize–winning investigative series on clinical laboratory testing.

The Bogdanich series was a broad investigation of laboratory quality based on interviews with patients, physicians, laboratory personnel, state regulators, private accreditors, and federal officials. This series provided a format for subsequent media treatments and congressional hearings by opening with a harrowing report of a death allegedly related to poor laboratory testing. Bogdanich's article related the story of Janice Johnson, a young mother who died of cervical cancer that had allegedly gone undetected due to erroneous reading of two Pap tests. The article suggested that the responsible laboratory was only one of thousands that were unlicensed and operated under a freedom from regulatory oversight that not even hairdressers enjoyed.

Bogdanich's series portrayed numerous cases of human tragedy for which victims claimed inaccurate laboratory testing: infant diseases that went undetected in prenatal testing, deaths from cancer that laboratory tests did not identify, marital breakups due to false-positive syphilis tests, and ruined careers from false-positive drug-test results. State regulatory bodies were charged with superficial and incomplete laboratory monitoring and inspection, and voluntary accrediting organizations were criticized for similar laxity. The series characterized the federal laboratory regulatory standards as "a surreal tangle of contradictory regulations."

The Bogdanich series was followed in 1987 by a prize-winning television series by investigative reporter Lea Thompson of Washington, D.C.'s WRC-TV. Her series investigated laboratory management based on Freedom of Information Act requests, analyses of test results, and interviews with physicians and laboratory personnel in nine states. The five-day series, "Deadly Mistakes," revealed instances of death and injury that victims believed were caused by false-negative tests and agonizing, unnecessary medical procedures they believed were ordered because of false-positive tests. This series highlighted Pap testing, which, Thompson charged, had an error rate of 20 to 40 percent.

Other media exposés followed these two major series, and on October 19, 1987, Congressman Ron Wyden's (D-Oreg.) House Subcommittee on Regulation and Business Opportunities held the first of numerous congressional hearings on laboratory quality. The Wyden hearing heard testimony from a variety of medical witnesses who alleged serious deficiencies in private laboratory testing for acquired immunodeficiency syndrome (AIDS).

Congressional hearings continued in 1988 with a January 28, 1988, session held by Senators Barbara Mikulski (D-Md.) and Brock Adams (D-Wash.) of the Senate Labor and Human Resources Committee. This laboratory quality hearing focused particularly on mistakes affecting women's health, especially those in Pap smear testing. Subsequently, further hearings were held by Congressman Wyden's Subcommittee and by

Congressman John Dingell's (D-Mich.) House Subcommittee on Oversight and Investigations of the Energy and Commerce Committee, and Senator Carl Levin's Subcommittee on Oversight of Governmental Management of the Senate Governmental Affairs Committee. All of these hearings revealed widespread errors in clinical laboratory testing and inadequate private-sector governmental oversight at both the federal and state level.

The media and congressional consensus from these hearings was that laboratory testing was plagued with errors, particularly in Pap testing, and that a more comprehensive and intensive scheme of quality regulation was necessary to change this dangerous situation.

Q.1:3 What is the stated purpose of CLIA'88?

The purpose of CLIA'88 was expressed in a congressional report as follows:

> The Clinical Laboratory Improvement Amendments of 1988 . . . resolve concerns that have been raised about deficiencies in the Clinical Laboratory Improvement Act of 1967. The legislation is intended to strengthen federal oversight of clinical laboratories to assure that the test results are accurate and reliable.
>
> Under the bill, all laboratories would be encompassed by a federal certification scheme. The role of private accrediting bodies would be clarified. New and more flexible enforcement authority would be granted to the Secretary [of the Department of Health and Human Services]. Requirements to assure the reliability of cytology screening would be mandated. Emphasis would be placed on the development and dissemination of information on laboratory quality. [House Rep. No. 100-899, 100th Cong., 2nd Sess. (Sept. 9, 1988) at 8]

In other words, the law was intended to give the federal government the responsibility, authority, and enforcement tools necessary to ensure that clinical laboratory testing produced accurate and reliable results throughout the United States.

Q.1:4 Which laboratories are covered by CLIA'88?

CLIA'88 and its implementing regulations, 42 C.F.R. Part 493, apply to all clinical laboratories in the United States (other than those specifically exempted), regardless of location or ownership. A *laboratory* or *clinical laboratory* is defined by the statute as follows:

> A facility for the biological, microbiological, serological, chemical, immunohematological, hematological, biophysical, cytological, pathological, or other examination of materials derived from the human body for the purpose of providing information for the diagnosis, prevention or treatment of any disease or impairment of, or the assessment of the health of, human beings. [42 U.S.C. §263a(a)]

Similarly, the regulations define *laboratory* as follows:

> Laboratory means a facility for the biological, microbiological, serological, chemical, immunohematological, hematological, biophysical, cytological, pathological, or other examination of materials derived from the human body for the purpose of providing information for the diagnosis, prevention or treatment of any disease or impairment of, or the assessment of the health of, human beings. These examinations also include procedures to determine, measure, or otherwise describe the presence or absence of various substances or organisms in the body. Facilities only collecting or preparing specimens (or both) or only serving as a mailing service and not performing testing are not considered laboratories. [42 C.F.R. §493.2]

CLIA'88 requires all clinical laboratories (other than those specifically exempted) to hold federally issued certificates in order to perform testing in the United States. The law establishes extensive standards that laboratories must meet to obtain such certification and prescribes penalties for testing without certification.

As explained by the Department of Health and Human Services, the CLIA'88 law and its implementing regulations apply to the following types of entities that perform test procedures or examinations. (This list is not all-inclusive; any entity falling within the above-quoted definition of *laboratory* is covered by CLIA'88.)

- Accredited hospital-based facilit[ies];
- Nonaccredited hospital-based facilit[ies];
- Federal hospitals, such as military, and Public Health Service hospitals;
- Independent laboratories;
- Critical care units;
- Physicians' office laboratories;
- Skilled nursing facilities;
- End-stage renal disease facilities;
- Intermediate care facilities, including intermediate care facilities for the mentally retarded;
- Laboratories associated with tissue banks and tissue repositories;
- Ambulatory surgical centers;
- Rural health clinics;
- Laboratory accreditation program of the College of American Pathologists (CAP) accredited, New York State approved, and low-volume exempt laboratories;
- Industrial laboratories that monitor employee health and test for drugs or abuse;
- Insurance company laboratories;
- City, state, and county laboratories;
- Planned Parenthood clinics;
- Mobile laboratories;

- Drug screening laboratories;
- Health maintenance organizations;
- Any other facility, including pharmacies and health fairs, that performs quantitative, qualitative, or screening test procedures or examinations. [57 Fed. Reg. 7007 (February 28, 1992)]

Q.1:5 Which laboratories are exempt from CLIA'88?

The laboratories that are specifically exempted from CLIA'88 are the following:

- Any facility or component of a facility that only performs testing for forensic purposes;
- Research laboratories that test human specimens but do not report patient-specific results for the diagnosis, prevention, or treatment of any disease or impairment of, or the assessment of, the health of individual patients; or
- Laboratories certified by the National Institutes on Drug Abuse (NIDA; see Chapter 10 of this *Answer Book*), in which drug testing is performed that meets NIDA guidelines and regulations; however, all other testing conducted by a NIDA-certified laboratory is subject to CLIA'88.

Q.1:6 Are any tests exempt from CLIA'88?

Under CLIA'88 and its implementing regulations, a laboratory may obtain a "certificate of waiver," meaning that it does not have to comply with CLIA'88's standards, if all the tests that the laboratory performs are among those classified as "waivered."

Waivered tests are defined as simple tests that have an insignificant risk of an erroneous result. These tests include the following:

- Tests approved for home use by the Food and Drug Administration (FDA);
- Tests that employ methods that are so simple and accurate that the likelihood of erroneous results is negligible; and

- Tests that pose no reasonable risk of harm to the patient if performed incorrectly. [42 C.F.R. §493.15]

Q.1:7 How does CLIA'88 relate to the Medicare and Medicaid programs?

CLIA'88 is a program of performance standards for clinical laboratories, whereas Medicare and Medicaid are insurance programs for the health care expenses of the aged and the poor, respectively. However, the standards for clinical laboratory participation in Medicare and Medicaid are the CLIA'88 standards.

Q.1:8 What are the "waivered" tests?

As of January 1, 1993, the list of waivered tests is as follows:

1. Dipstick or tablet reagent urinalysis (nonautomated) for the following:
   (i) Bilirubin,
   (ii) Glucose,
   (iii) Hemoglobin,
   (iv) Ketone,
   (v) Leukocytes,
   (vi) Nitrite,
   (vii) pH,
   (viii) Protein,
   (ix) Specific gravity, and
   (x) Urobilinogen;
2. Fecal occult blood;
3. Ovulation tests—visual color comparison tests for human luteinizing hormone;
4. Urine pregnancy tests—visual color comparison tests;
5. Erythrocyte sedimentation rate—nonautomated;
6. Hemoglobin—copper sulfate—nonautomated;

7. Blood glucose by glucose monitoring devices cleared by the FDA specifically for home use; and
8. Spun microhematocrit. [42 C.F.R. §493.15]

Q.1:9 Does CLIA'88 differentiate among laboratories by site?

CLIA'88 does not differentiate among laboratories by site. Rather, CLIA'88 differentiates among laboratories according to the degree of complexity of the tests they perform. The CLIA'88 regulations are based on a "complexity model" that establishes different regulatory standards for tests classified as "moderate complexity" than for tests classified as "high complexity." Performance standards under CLIA'88 differ depending on whether the laboratory conducts moderate- or high-complexity tests.

Q.1:10 How does the CLIA'88 "complexity model" work?

The model classifies each specific test system, assay, and examination by complexity in the following way. There are seven criteria for complexity in the model. Each clinical laboratory test is graded for level of complexity by assigning the score of 1, 2, or 3 within each criterion. The score 1 indicates the lowest level of complexity, and the score 3 indicates the highest level. Then the scores for all of the criteria are totaled for each test. If the test's total score is 12 or fewer, it will be categorized as "moderate complexity," while if the score is greater than 12, the test will be categorized as "high complexity."

Q.1:11 What are the seven criteria used in the CLIA'88 complexity model?

The seven criteria used in the CLIA'88 complexity model are as follows:

1. Knowledge: The degree of scientific and technical knowledge that is required to perform the test.

2. Training and experience: The degree of experience required for the preanalytic, analytic, and postanalytic phases of the testing process.
3. Reagents and the materials preparation: Whether the reagents and materials used in the test process or system are generally stable and reliable, or, on the other hand, require any special handling, precautions, or storage conditions to ensure reliablity for manual steps in the testing process.
4. Characteristics of the operational steps: Whether the operational steps in the testing process are easily controlled or automatically executed, on the one hand, or require close monitoring or control, special specimen preparation, temperature control, timing, extensive calculations, and so forth, on the other hand.
5. Calibration, quality control, and proficiency testing materials: Whether these materials are stable and readily available, on the one hand, or are labile or not available, on the other.
6. A test system trouble shooting and equipment maintenance: Whether test system trouble shooting is automatic or self-correcting, or requires minimal judgment, on the one hand, or is not automatic and requires decision making and direct intervention to solve problems, on the other.
7. Interpretation and judgment: Whether minimal interpretation and judgment are required to perform preanalytic, analytic, and postanalytic processes and resolve problems, on the one hand, or whether extensive interpretation and judgment are required to perform the testing processes and resolve problems, on the other.

Q.1:12 What is the list of tests classified as "moderate complexity"?

The generic list of tests classified as "moderate complexity," as issued in the Preamble to the CLIA '88 regulations, is as follows:

(1) Clinical cytogenetics
    (i) No procedures.
(2) Histopathology
    (i) No procedures.

(3) Histocompatibility
- (i) No procedures.

(4) Cytology
- (i) No procedures.

(5) Bacteriology
- (i) Primary culture inoculation;
- (ii) Urine culture and colony count kits;
- (iii) Microscopic evaluation of direct wet mount preparations;
- (iv) Isolation and presumptive identification of aerobic bacteria from throat or urine or cervical/urethral specimens;
- (v) Isolation and confirmatory identification of aerobic bacteria from throat or urine or cervical/urethral specimens;
- (vi) Gram stain;
- (vii) Darkfield examination for *Treponema pallidum*;
- (viii) Manual procedures with limited steps and with limited sample or reagent preparation;
- (ix) Manual screening devices for bacteriuria with limited steps and with limited sample or reagent preparation; and
- (x) Automated procedures that do not require intervention during the analytic process.

(6) Mycobacteriology
- (i) Direct acid fast smear.

(7) Mycology
- (i) Primary culture inoculation;
- (ii) Isolation of yeast with identification limited to *Candida albicans;*
- (iii) Identification procedures for *Candida albicans* (excluding semiautomated and semiquantitative procedures);
- (iv) Microscopic evaluation of direct wet mount preparations;
- (v) Tests using selective media for the presence or absence of dermatophytes;

(vi) Microscopic evaluation of KOH [potassium hydroxide] preparations;
(vii) Manual procedures with limited steps and with limited sample or reagent preparation; and
(viii) Automated mycology procedures that do not require operator intervention during the analytic process.

(8) Parasitology
(i) Microscopic evaluation of pinworm preparations;
(ii) Microscopic evaluation of direct wet mount preparations for the presence or absence of parasites;
(iii) Manual procedures with limited steps and with limited sample or reagent preparation; and
(iv) Culture devices indicating the presence or absence of *Trichomonas vaginalis*.

(9) Virology
(i) Manual procedures with limited steps and with limited sample or reagent preparation; and
(ii) Automated procedures that do not require operator intervention during the analytic process.

(10) Immunology
(i) Automated procedures that do not require operator intervention during the analytic process;
(ii) Darkfield examinations for *Treponema pallidum*; and
(iii) Manual procedures with limited steps and with limited sample or reagent preparation.

(11) Chemistry (Routine/Endocrinology/Toxicology)
(i) Automated procedures that do not require operator intervention during the analytic process;
(ii) Automated blood gas analyses that do not require operator intervention during the analytic process (such as instruments that have an automated process for calibration, sample intake, and flushing of sample lines);

(iii) Whole blood measurements using test stripmeters (excluding glucose monitoring devices cleared by the FDA specifically for home use);
(iv) Osmolality measurements; and
(v) Manual procedures with limited steps and with limited sample or reagent preparation.

(12) Urinalysis
(i) Microscopic analysis of urinary sediment; and
(ii) Automated urinalysis procedures that do not require operator intervention during the analytic process.

(13) Hematology
(i) Automated hematology procedures without differentials that do not require operator intervention during the analytic process;
(ii) Automated hematology procedures with differentials that do not require operator intervention during the analytic process and that do not require an analyst to interpret a histogram or scattergram;
(iii) Manual white blood cell differential counts when the analyst is not required to identify atypical cells;
(iv) Automated procedures that do not require operator intervention during the analytic process;
(v) Manual hematology procedures with limited steps and with limited sample or reagent preparation; and
(vi) Manual coagulation procedures with limited steps and with limited sample or reagent preparation.

(14) Immunohematology
(i) Manual or semiautomated procedures with limited steps and with limited sample or reagent preparation; and
(ii) Automated procedures that do not require operator intervention during the analytic process.

(15) Other
- (i) Semen analysis for the presence or absence of sperm;
- (ii) Occult blood on body fluids;
- (iii) Crystal analyses on joint fluid; and
- (iv) Viscosity. [57 Fed. Reg. 7018 (Feb. 28, 1992)]

Q.1:13 What is the list of tests classified as "high complexity"?

The generic list of tests classified as "high complexity," as issued in the Preamble to the CLIA '88 regulations, is as follows:

(1) Clinical cytogenetics
- (i) All procedures.

(2) Histopathology
- (i) All procedures.

(3) Histocompatibility
- (i) All procedures.

(4) Cytology
- (i) All procedures.

(5) Bacteriology
- (i) Isolation and identification of aerobic and anaerobic bacteria from specimens that are not specified in moderate complexity;
- (ii) Automated or semiautomated procedures that do not require operator intervention during the analytic process;
- (iii) Serogrouping/typing;
- (iv) Antigen or toxin test procedures or kits requiring microscopic evaluation;
- (v) Manual procedures with multiple steps in sample or reagent preparation or the analytic process; and
- (vi) Semiautomated nonculture urine screening devices predicting bacteriuria.

(6) Mycobacteriology
- (i) Concentration, smear, and primary culture inoculation;

- (ii) Isolation and identification techniques;
- (iii) Antimycobacterial susceptibility testing;
- (iv) Manual procedures with multiple steps in sample or reagent preparation or the analytic process; and
- (v) Automated or semiautomated procedures that do not require operator intervention during the analytic process.

(7) Mycology

- (i) Isolation and identification of all fungi not specified in moderate complexity;
- (ii) Identification techniques requiring interpretative skills;
- (iii) Automated or semiautomated mycology procedures that do not require operator intervention during the analytic process; and
- (iv) Manual procedures with multiple steps in sample or reagent preparation or the analytic process.

(8) Parasitology

- (i) Identification techniques requiring interpretative skills;
- (ii) Concentration or differential staining techniques;
- (iii) Antigen test procedures or kits requiring microscopic evaluation; and
- (iv) Manual procedures with multiple steps in sample or reagent preparation or the analytic process.

(9) Virology

- (i) Isolation and identification techniques;
- (ii) Antigen test procedures or kits requiring microscopic evaluation;
- (iii) Manual procedures with multiple steps, in sample or reagent preparation or the analytic process; and
- (iv) Automated or semiautomated procedures that do not require operator intervention during the analytic process.

(10) Immunology
- (i) Gel-based immunochemical procedures;
- (ii) Electrophoresis;
- (iii) Western blot;
- (iv) Immunoassay procedures requiring microscopic evaluations;
- (v) Procedures requiring cell or tissue culture techniques;
- (vi) Automated or semiautomated procedures that do not require operator intervention during the analytic process;
- (vii) Cell phenotyping and analysis;
- (viii) Radioimmunoassays; and
- (ix) Manual procedures with multiple steps in sample or reagent preparation or the analytic process.

(11) Chemistry (Routine/Endocrinology/Toxicology)
- (i) Manual procedures with multiple steps in sample or reagent preparation or the analytic process;
- (ii) Atomic absorption;
- (iii) Flame photometry;
- (iv) Electrophoresis;
- (v) Gel-based immunochemical procedures;
- (vi) Blood gas analyses that do not require operator intervention to calibrate the instrument, equilibrate gas supplies, introduce samples into measuring chambers, or flush sample lines;
- (vii) Automated or semiautomated procedures that do require operator intervention during the analytic process;
- (viii) Anodic stripping voltometry;
- (ix) Radioimmunoassays; and
- (x) Mass spectrometry.

(12) Urinalysis
- (i) Automated or semiautomated procedures that do require operator intervention during the analytic process.

(13) Hematology
- (i) Manual reticulocyte counts;
- (ii) Hemoglobin electrophoresis;
- (iii) Bone marrow evaluation;
- (iv) Manual coagulation procedures with multiple steps in sample or reagent preparation or the analytic process;
- (v) Manual cell counts;
- (vi) Automated or semiautomated procedures that do require operator intervention during the analytic process;
- (vii) Manual white blood cell differential counts when the analyst is required to identify atypical cells;
- (viii) Manual hematology procedures with multiple steps in sample or reagent preparation or the analytic process;
- (ix) Flow cytometry; and
- (x) Manual platelet counts.

(14) Immunohematology
- (i) Manual procedures with multiple steps in sample or reagent preparation or the analytic process;
- (ii) Semiautomated and automated procedures that do require operator intervention during the analytic process; and
- (iii) Compatibility testing (includes any of the following when performed in the process of determining donor/recipient compatibility: recipient and donor ABO group/D(Rho) type/special antigen typing; direct antiglobulin test; tests for unexpected antibody detection and identification; crossmatch procedures).

(15) Other
- (i) Semen analysis (quantitative); and
- (ii) Eye bank microscopy procedures. [57 Fed. Reg. 7018-7019 (Feb. 28, 1992)]

Q.1:14 What aspects of laboratory performance are covered by CLIA'88?

CLIA'88 and its implementing regulations cover the full spectrum of clinical laboratory functions, including the following:

- Personnel qualifications and duties;
- Patient test management;
- Facilities, equipment, and supplies;
- Quality control;
- Quality assurance;
- Record keeping; and
- Proficiency testing.

Q.1:15 Which federal agency administers and enforces CLIA'88?

CLIA'88 is administered and enforced by the Department of Health and Human Services (HHS), specifically by HHS' Health Care Financing Administration (HCFA) and Public Health Service (PHS).

Q.1:16 Are any of the CLIA'88 standards specialty-specific?

Yes. CLIA'88 requirements in the area of quality control are specific to the following laboratory specialties:

- Microbiology,
- Bacteriology,
- Mycobacteriology,
- Mycology,
- Parasitology,
- Virology,
- Diagnostic immunology,

- Syphilis serology,
- General immunology,
- Chemistry,
- Routine chemistry,
- Endocrinology,
- Toxicology,
- Hematology,
- Pathology,
- Cytology,
- Histopathology,
- Oral pathology,
- Radiobioassay,
- Histocompatibility,
- Clinical cytogenetics,
- Immunohematology, and
- Transfusion services and blood banking.

Additionally, CLIA'88's proficiency testing requirements vary by specialty. See **Q.1:21**, below.

Q.1:17 Are there any laboratory specialties that have unique performance standards under CLIA'88?

Yes. CLIA'88 establishes special performance standards for certain aspects of cytology testing, in large part due to congressional hearings and media investigations that preceded the enactment of CLIA'88 and revealed substantial error rates in cytology testing in many areas of the United States. (See **Q1:2**, above.) CLIA'88's cytology standards are intended, at least in part, to address a problem that congressional hearings and media exposés linked to these high cytology error rates: the very high volumes of cytology slides that laboratory technicians examined per day, week, or month.

Q.1:18 What types of requirements are included in CLIA'88's cytology standards?

The quality control requirements for the specialty of cytology in the CLIA'88 regulations are considerably more extensive than the quality control requirements for other specialties addressed in the regulations. Among the requirements for cytology testing are the following:

- The laboratory must ensure that there are effective measures to prevent cross-contamination between gynecologic and nongynecologic specimens during the staining process.
- The laboratory must ensure that there are no interpretations reported on smears that are unsatisfactory.
- All cytology slide preparations must be evaluated on the laboratory premises.
- Strict workload limitations must be observed: each individual evaluating cytology preparations by nonautomated microscopic techniques can examine no more than 100 slides in each 24-hour period, regardless of the site or sites where the examinations occur; the regulations emphasize that the 100-slide limitation is "an absolute maximum" that is not to be used as a "performance target."
- Records must be maintained of the total number of slides examined by each individual during each 24-hour period, regardless of the site where the examinations occur, as well as the number of hours each individual spends examining slides in the 24-hour period.
- The 100-slide workload limitation must occur in no less than an eight-hour workday.
- All gynecologic smears that are interpreted to show reactive or reparative changes, atypical squamous or glandular cells of undetermined significance, or to be in the premalignant or malignant category must be confirmed by a technical supervisor in cytology, and the report must be signed to reflect the review.
- All nongynecologic cytologic preparations must be reviewed by the technical supervisor in cytology, and the report must be signed to reflect the review.
- The performance of each cytotechnologist in slide examination must be evaluated and documented.

- The technical supervisor must establish a maximum number of slides for each individual examining slide preparations by nonautomated, microscopic technique, and the maximum for each individual may not exceed the 100-slide maximum workload limit.
- The laboratory must establish and follow a program designed to detect errors in the performance of cytologic examinations and the reporting of cytologic results, following specific program criteria identified in the regulations.
- In reporting cytology test results, the laboratory must clearly distinguish specimens, smears, or both that are unsatisfactory for diagnostic interpretation and must use narrative, descriptive nomenclature for all results.
- Any corrected reports issued by the laboratory must indicate the basis for the correction.
- The laboratory must retain all slide preparations for five years from the date of examination or, alternatively, must loan slides to proficiency testing programs in lieu of maintaining the slides for the five-year time period, as long as the laboratory receives written acknowledgment that the proficiency testing program has received the slides and the laboratory maintains this written acknowledgment to document the loan of the slides.

Q.1:19 What proficiency testing requirements must laboratories observe under CLIA'88?

Among the proficiency testing requirements that all laboratories must follow under CLIA'88 are the following:

- Each laboratory must enroll in a proficiency testing (PT) program approved by HHS for each of the specialties and subspecialties in which the laboratory is to be certified.
- PT samples must be tested in the same manner as patient specimens are tested.

- The laboratory must authorize each PT program in which it participates to release to HHS all data required to assess the laboratory's PT performance and make PT results available to the public pursuant to the CLIA'88 regulations.
- PT samples must be tested with the laboratory's regular patient workload, by personnel who routinely perform the testing in the laboratory, using the laboratory's routine testing methods.
- The individual who tests PT samples and the laboratory director must attest that the samples have been integrated into the patient workload using the laboratory's routine methods;
- PT samples must be tested for the same number of times that the laboratory routinely tests patient samples.
- Laboratories performing tests on PT samples must not engage in any interlaboratory communications about the results of PT samples until after the date by which the laboratory must report PT results to the program for the testing event in which the samples were sent.
- Laboratories with multiple testing sites or locations must not conduct intersite communications concerning PT results until after the date by which the laboratory must report PT results to the program.
- Laboratories must not send PT samples or parts of samples to any other laboratory for any analysis that the original laboratory is certified to perform; the penalty for such referral of PT specimens is the revocation of CLIA'88 certification for at least one year, and any laboratory receiving referrals of PT samples must notify HHS of the receipt.
- The laboratory must document the handling, preparation, processing, examination, and each step in the testing and reporting of results for all PT samples, and must maintain a copy of all records for a minimum of two years from the date of the PT event.

Q.1:20 How is successful participation in proficiency testing defined by CLIA'88?

The CLIA'88 regulations define "unsuccessful proficiency testing performance" as follows: "A failure to attain the minimum satisfactory score for an analyte, test, subspecialty or specialty for two consecutive or two of three consecutive testing events. [42 C.F.R. §493.2]

Q.1:21 What is the minimum satisfactory score in a proficiency testing event?

Minimum satisfactory scores in PT events are defined separately for the following specialties and subspecialties:

- Microbiology,
- Bacteriology,
- Mycobacteriology,
- Mycology,
- Parasitology,
- Virology,
- Diagnostic immunology,
- Syphilis serology,
- General immunology,
- Chemistry,
- Routine chemistry,
- Endocrinology,
- Toxicology,
- Hematology,
- Cytology; and
- Immunohematology.

For most specialties, failure to attain an overall testing event score of at least 80 percent is unsatisfactory performance.

Q.1:22 What standards must a proficiency testing program meet in order to be approved by HHS?

In order for a PT program to be approved by HHS, the program must meet the following standards:

- Be offered by a private, nonprofit organization or a federal or state agency, or an entity acting as a designated agent for a state;
- Submit an application providing required information by July 1 of the year preceding the year for which approval is requested;
- Provide technical assistance to laboratories that seek to qualify under the program;
- For each specialty, subspecialty, and analyte or test covered by the program, ensure the quality of test samples, appropriately evaluate and score the testing results, and identify performance problems in a timely manner;
- For each specialty, subspecialty, analyte, or test covered by the program, demonstrate to HHS that the program has the technical ability required to prepare or purchase samples from manufacturers who prepare the samples in conformance with regulatory Good Manufacturing Practices established by the Food and Drug Administration;
- For each specialty, subspecialty, analyte, or test covered, demonstrate to HHS that the program has the ability to distribute the samples, using rigorous quality control to ensure that they mimic actual patient samples when possible and that they are homogenous and will be stable within the timeframe for analysis by program participants;
- Demonstrate to HHS that the program has a scientifically defensible process for determining the correct result for each challenge offered;
- Demonstrate to HHS that the program has a schedule of sufficient annual challenge, according to frequencies specified in the regulations, to establish that a laboratory has met minimum performance requirements;
- Demonstrate to HHS that the program has the resources needed to provide statewide or nationwide reports to regulatory agencies on individual performance for gynecologic cytology and individual laboratory performance on testing events, cumulative reports and scores for each laboratory or individual, and reports of specific laboratory failures, all on a timely basis;

- Demonstrate to HHS that it has provisions to include on each PT report form used by the laboratory an attestation that PT samples were treated in the same manner as patient samples;
- Demonstrate to HHS that the program has a mechanism for notifying participants of the PT shipping schedule and for participants to notify the program within three days of the expected date of receipt of the shipment that samples have not arrived or are unacceptable, and for replacing unacceptable samples;
- Demonstrate to HHS that the program has a process to resolve technical, administrative, and scientific problems about program operations;
- Meet specific criteria for PT programs in each specialty and subspecialty covered by the CLIA'88 regulations; and
- Comply with packaging and shipping requirements set forth at 42 C.F.R. Part 72.

Q.1:23 What sanctions does CLIA'88 prescribe for failure to participate successfully in PT?

Failure to participate successfully in PT is considered to be a "condition level" violation of CLIA'88 that is subject to the principal CLIA'88 sanctions (suspension, limitation, or revocation of any type of CLIA'88 certificate) or alternative sanctions including a directed plan of correction, state on-site monitoring, or civil money penalties.

It should also be noted that laboratories can be sanctioned for referring PT samples to another laboratory for testing. (See **Q.1:19**, above.)

Q.1:24 What must a laboratory do in order to be reinstated with CLIA certification and participation in Medicare or Medicaid after failing to participate successfully in PT?

If a laboratory loses its CLIA'88 certification (and/or Medicare or Medicaid approval) as a result of failure to participate successfully in PT, the laboratory must then demonstrate sustained satisfactory performance on two consecutive PT events in order to be considered for reinstatement in the affected specialty, subspecialty, analyte, or test.

In any event, the loss of certification and/or Medicare or Medicaid approval for PT failure will be not less than six months from the date of termination.

However, if the laboratory loses its certification and/or Medicare or Medicaid approval in the specialty of gynecologic cytology, in order to be reinstated, the laboratory must take specific corrective action and formally reapply for certification in that specialty.

Q.1:25 What requirements concerning the educational and/or experiential qualifications of laboratory personnel does CLIA'88 impose?

The CLIA'88 statute and implementing regulations link personnel requirements to the complexity of testing. The requirements differ substantially for personnel who perform moderate- versus high-complexity testing and thus are defined separately for the two categories of tests. The regulations list specific qualifications for the various positions within a laboratory and define the functions and responsibilities of the persons who fill these positions. Persons who are qualified may perform the functions of more than one position in either moderate- or high-complexity testing. For example, the same person may function as both the laboratory director and the clinical consultant. In a few cases, one person could qualify and function in all of the positions listed.

Q.1:26 For what laboratory positions do the CLIA'88 personnel regulations prescribe qualifications and functions?

For laboratories performing moderate-complexity testing, the CLIA'88 regulations specify qualifications and functions for the following positions:

- Laboratory director,
- Technical consultant,
- Clinical consultant, and
- Testing personnel.

For laboratories performing high-complexity testing, the CLIA'88 regulations set out qualifications and functions for the following positions:

- Laboratory director,
- Technical supervisor,
- Clinical consultant,
- General supervisor,
- Cytology general supervisor,
- Cytotechnologist, and
- Testing personnel.

Q.1:27 How does the CLIA'88 certification process work?

The CLIA'88 certification process works as follows. First, the laboratory must obtain from HHS either a certificate of waiver (if it performs only tests in the waivered category), or, if a laboratory performs nonwaivered testing, a registration certificate. Information and an application for a registration certificate will either be sent to the laboratory or can be obtained from the HCFA office in the region where the laboratory operates. Registration certificates are valid for a maximum of two years or until such time as an inspection can be conducted to determine compliance with the CLIA'88 program, whichever is shorter.

Once an inspection is conducted, the laboratory will be issued either a certificate, for a laboratory complying directly with the CLIA'88 program run by HHS, or a certificate of accreditation, issued to those laboratories that choose to comply with private nonprofit accreditation programs approved by HHS as having standards that are equivalent to CLIA'88's. In addition, in states with federally approved licensure programs, a laboratory may obtain a state license in lieu of a certificate or a certificate of accreditation. If the laboratory is located in a state with an approved program and the laboratory obtains a state license, it only has to comply with the state rules, not the federal CLIA'88 regulations.

Q.1:28 What is the role of accreditation under CLIA'88?

The CLIA'88 law provides that a laboratory may obtain a CLIA'88 certificate of accreditation if it meets the standards of an accreditation program that has been approved by HHS and if the laboratory authorizes the accrediting organization to submit to HHS records or other information that HHS requires.

The CLIA'88 regulations provide that, in order to be deemed in compliance with CLIA'88, a laboratory accredited by an approved accrediting organization must also do the following:

- Authorize the accrediting organization to release to HHS all records and information required by HHS,
- Permit inspections pursuant to CLIA'88 requirements,
- Obtain a certificate of accreditation from the approved accrediting organization, and
- Pay applicable fees.

Q.1:29 What must an accrediting body do in order to be approved by HHS under CLIA'88?

In order to be approved by HHS under CLIA'88, a private accrediting organization must meet the following requirements:

- Provide reasonable assurance to HHS that it requires accredited laboratories to meet all requirements of its program that are equal to CLIA'88 "condition-level" requirements;
- Be accountable for the monitoring of laboratory compliance with CLIA'88 standards;

- Be determined to be acceptable by HHS after an evaluation process that covers, among other things, the equivalency of the accrediting organization's requirements with CLIA'88 condition-level standards; the organization's inspection process; the comparability of the organization's inspection and complaint follow-up process to HHS'; the organization's procedures for monitoring laboratories that are found out of compliance with its requirements; the organization's ability to provide data on its inspection process and PT results in appropriate electronic format; and the adequacy of the organization's staff and funding;
- Inspect laboratories for accreditation purposes at a frequency determined by HHS, using inspectors qualified to evaluate laboratory methodologies and test procedures;
- Apply standards equal to or more stringent than HHS CLIA'88 certification standards;
- Provide adequate assurance that these standards continue to be satisfied by the laboratories that the organization accredits;
- Submit to HHS the name of any laboratory that has had its accreditation denied, suspended, withdrawn, or revoked, or that has been the subject of any other adverse action by the accreditation organization, within 30 days of such action;
- Notify HHS at least 30 days before changing accreditation standards;
- Notify each laboratory accredited within ten days of a decision by HHS to withdraw the organization's accreditation approval;
- Provide HCFA with inspection schedules, on request for the purpose of conducting on-site validation inspections; and
- Provide HHS with facility-specific data on request, including information on PT results and related adverse actions.

Q.1:30 How long does HHS approval of accrediting organizations under CLIA'88 last?

The maximum period for which HHS may approve an accrediting organization under CLIA'88 is six years.

Q.1:31 What private accrediting bodies and state organizations have been approved to administer CLIA'88?

As of December 31, 1992, the following private accrediting organizations and state licensure programs were approved by HCFA:

- American Association of Bioanalysts (800/234-5315);
- American Association for Clinical Chemistry (800/892-1400);
- American Proficiency Institute (800/333-0958);
- American Thoracic Society (212/315-8808 or 8789);
- California Thoracic Society (714/730-1944);
- New York Department of Health (518/474-8739);
- New Jersey Department of Health (609/530-6172);
- Idaho Department of Health (208/334-2235);
- College of American Pathologists (CAP) (800/323-4040);
- American Society of Internal Medicine (800/338-2746);
- American Academy of Family Physicians (800/274-2237); and
- EXCEL Program, CAP (800/323-4040).

Q.1:32 Does CLIA'88 require laboratories to pay fees for certification?

Yes. Under CLIA'88, HHS must require laboratories to pay fees for the issuance and renewal of laboratory certificates. The fees are intended to earn sufficient revenues to cover the federal government's general costs of administering the CLIA'88 regulatory program, including the costs of HHS inspections and PT. However, fees for issuance and renewal of certificates of waiver are required by law to be nominal.

The CLIA'88 regulations at 42 C.F.R. §§493.602–649 specify the fees for registration certificates and certificates. These fees vary according to the numbers of specialties in which the laboratory performs and the volume of testing the laboratory performs. For more detailed information on CLIA'88 fees, see L.R.M., Part 6.1, Section 3-8.

Q.1:33 How long do CLIA'88 certificates last?

Under the CLIA'88 law and regulations, CLIA'88 certificates are valid for no more than two years. [See 42 C.F.R. §§493.35–63.]

Q.1:34 Can inspections under CLIA'88 occur on an unannounced basis?

Yes. The CLIA'88 statute permits HHS to conduct unannounced inspections to verify compliance with the law. In establishing its CLIA'88 regulatory program, HHS has decided that it will conduct unannounced inspections. During an inspection, the laboratory must allow the inspectors to have access to all areas of the facility, observe employees performing tests or other functions, interview employees, and review records. A laboratory that refuses to permit an inspection will be subject to suspension of its CLIA certification or its participation in the Medicare program.

Q.1:35 What sanctions can be imposed for violation of CLIA'88 requirements?

Under the CLIA'88 regulations, HHS may impose sanctions against laboratories for failure to comply with CLIA'88 requirements. CLIA'88 requirements are classified as either "condition level" or "standard level." For violations that are considered to be condition level, in the case of one or more violations, HCFA may impose any of the following three principal CLIA sanctions:

1. Suspension of a certificate for a period of time,
2. Limitation of the scope of a certificate, or
3. Revocation of a certificate.

Alternatively, HHS may impose one or more alternative sanctions in lieu of or in addition to a principal sanction (except on a laboratory that has a certificate of waiver). The alternative sanctions include the following three:

1. Directed plans of correction,
2. State on-site monitoring, or
3. Civil money penalties.

In addition, HHS may suspend all or part of Medicare or Medicaid payment.

HHS may also enjoin a laboratory from continuing any activity that constitutes a significant hazard to the public health. Additionally, HHS may prohibit any person who owned or operated a laboratory that had its CLIA'88 certification revoked from owning or operating a laboratory within two years of the revocation.

When noncompliance with CLIA'88 is determined to pose immediate jeopardy to laboratory patients or the general public, HHS may suspend or limit the CLIA'88 certificate *before* holding a hearing. For nonimmediate jeopardy situations, HHS must conduct a hearing before sanctions can be imposed.

Q.1:36 Are there any types of violations that are treated differently or more severely than others?

Yes. As noted in **Q.1:35**, above, any noncompliance that is determined to pose immediate jeopardy to laboratory patients or the general public can be the cause for the suspension of a laboratory's CLIA'88 certificate immediately, without a hearing by HHS. Otherwise, HHS must hold a hearing before sanctions can be imposed.

Q.1:37 What is the effect on a laboratory's Medicare approval of an adverse action under CLIA'88?

When HCFA suspends or revokes any type of CLIA'88 certificate, the agency concurrently cancels the laboratory's approval to receive Medicare payment for its services. Similarly, when HCFA limits any type of CLIA'88 certificate, the agency concurrently limits the laboratory's Medicare approval to only those specialties or subspecialties of testing that the laboratory can continue to perform under the terms of its limited CLIA'88 certificate.

Q.1:38 How large are the civil money penalties that can be imposed on laboratories for violating CLIA'88 requirements?

The range of civil money penalty amounts that can be imposed under CLIA'88 is as follows. For a condition-level deficiency that poses immediate jeopardy to the public health, the range of potential penalties is $3,050 to $10,000 per day of noncompliance or per violation.

For a condition-level deficiency that does not pose immediate jeopardy to the public health, the range of potential civil money penalties is $50 to $3,000 per day of noncompliance or per violation. In a case where an immediate jeopardy is removed, but the deficiency continues, the penalty amount will be shifted to the lower range.

Q.1:39 What are the factors considered in determining the amount of the civil money penalty?

In determining the amount of the civil money penalty, HCFA will take into account the following factors:

- The nature, scope, severity, and duration of the noncompliance;
- Whether the same condition-level deficiencies have been identified during three consecutive inspections;
- The laboratory's overall compliance history, including, but not limited to, any period of noncompliance that occurred between certifications;
- The laboratory's intent or reason for noncompliance; and
- The accuracy and extent of laboratory records and their availability to inspection and enforcement personnel.

Q.1:40 What is the process by which a laboratory responds to an accusation of violating CLIA'88?

A laboratory will generally be able to respond to an accusation of violating CLIA'88 in an administrative hearing. Unless HCFA proposes a sanction in order to correct a condition that poses immediate jeopardy to laboratory patients or the general public, the sanction will not take effect until after the laboratory has had the opportunity for a hearing before an administrative law judge (ALJ). The ALJ's decision may be appealed to the HHS Departmental Appeals Board. That decision, if it concerns the imposition of a civil money penalty or the suspension or limitation of a CLIA certificate, may be appealed to a court. [See 42 C.F.R. §493.1844.]

Q.1:41 If a laboratory is sanctioned under CLIA'88, will it automatically lose its state license?

No. The imposition of a sanction under the federal CLIA'88 statute is not automatically grounds for the revocation or limitation of a state license. A state license may not be revoked after a CLIA'88 sanction unless the state authorities take action on their own. However, since the suspension or revocation of a CLIA'88 certificate means that a laboratory cannot perform testing in the United States, the state license is of little value when a CLIA'88 suspension or revocation is in effect.

Q.1:42 How does CLIA'88 relate to state laws in general?

CLIA'88 provides that no state is to be prevented from taking any action or enforcing any laws to the extent that such laws are not inconsistent with CLIA'88 or its implementing regulations.

In addition, under certain conditions, HHS may exempt laboratories in a state from compliance with CLIA'88 and its regulations. In order for a state's program to be exempt, the state must do the following:

- Show that its program has standards equal to or more stringent than CLIA'88's;
- Agree to finance a validation program run by HCFA;

- Agree to pay the state's *pro rata* share of the general costs of administering CLIA'88;
- Agree to take enforcement action against laboratories that violate significant requirements; and
- Allow HHS to inspect facilities in the state.

Q.1:43 How long does the exemption of a state program under CLIA'88 last?

HHS may exempt a state program from CLIA'88 requirements for up to six years.

Q.1:44 Are there any states whose laboratory programs have been exempted under this program?

Yes. In 1993, the state of Washington's program was exempted.

Q.1:45 How does CLIA'88 address new technology in laboratory testing?

In order to permit the CLIA'88 regulatory program to keep pace with changing technology, the CLIA'88 regulations provide for the creation of a committee of experts in laboratory medicine called the Clinical Laboratory Improvement Advisory Committee (CLIAC). This committee is made up of persons involved in the provision, utilization, and development of laboratory testing. Its duties are as follows:

- Advise and make recommendations on the technical and scientific aspects of the regulations;
- Review and make recommendations on criteria for categorizing tests, personnel, patient test managements, PT, quality control and quality assurance, and other relevant issues; and

- Assist HHS in keeping the CLIA'88 regulations up to date with changing laboratory technology.

HHS has designated subcommittees of CLIAC to address particular issues. CLIAC or its subcommittees are required to meet at least once a year. (See 42 C.F.R. §493.2001.)

Q.1:46 Does CLIA'88 include provisions to give the laboratory industry a role in the administration or revision of CLIA'88 requirements?

Yes. The CLIA'88 statute permits HHS, in carrying out its responsibilities, to "consult with appropriate private organizations and public agencies." [42 U.S.C. §263a(q)] HHS has implemented this provision by including persons "involved in the provision of laboratory services" in the membership of CLIAC. [42 C.F.R. §493.2001]

2

Medicare Reimbursement for Clinical Laboratory Tests

Q.2:1 What is Medicare?

Medicare is a federal program that provides health care insurance for persons 65 years of age and over and disabled persons, regardless of financial status. The program is structured in two parts. Part A provides for hospital and institutional care and is financed by employer/employee contributions into the Social Security system and federal matching funds. Part B provides for physicians' services; extended care outside institutions; and other medical services and supplies, including clinical laboratory tests. Part B is financed in part by beneficiary premium payments and payments from the General Fund of the U.S. Treasury.

Q.2:2 What individuals are eligible to receive Medicare benefits?

An individual is eligible for Medicare benefits if he or she is age 65 or over, or is disabled (defined as having received Social Security or Railroad Retirement disability benefits for 25 months), or has end-stage renal disease. [42 C.F.R. §406.5]

Q.2:3 What requirements must laboratories meet to provide services to Medicare beneficiaries?

In order to be qualified to participate in the Medicare program, a clinical laboratory must meet the standards for laboratory performance set forth at 42 C.F.R. Part 493, the CLIA'88 implementing regulations. (See Chapter 1.) Thus, the standards that laboratories must meet to participate in Medicare are the same standards that laboratories must meet under CLIA'88.

Q.2:4 Are there any limitations on the types of laboratory tests for which Medicare will provide reimbursement?

Yes. Medicare will not reimburse for, or "cover," clinical laboratory tests that are provided for screening purposes rather than to confirm or deny a particular suspected diagnosis. In addition, Medicare covers no item or service if it is not "reasonable and necessary for the diagnosis or treatment" of a particular condition. [42 U.S.C. §1395y(a)(1)] Thus, if a particular test is not "reasonable and necessary" for the particular patient's suspected diagnosis, or for any possible diagnosis or condition, then Medicare will not provide reimbursement.

Q.2:5 How does Medicare relate to CLIA'88?

Medicare is a program of federally financed medical insurance for the aged and disabled, whereas CLIA'88 is a program of quality regulation applicable to all clinical laboratories operating in the United States. However, the laboratory performance standards set forth in the CLIA'88 implementing regulations at 42 C.F.R. Part 493 are the same standards that laboratories must meet to participate in the Medicare program. Consequently, if a laboratory's CLIA'88 certification (see Chapter 1) is revoked or suspended, the laboratory's participation in the Medicare program will also be revoked or suspended until the laboratory regains its CLIA certification.

Q.2:6 What agency or agencies administer Medicare reimbursement for clinical laboratory tests?

Overall, the Medicare program is administered by the Health Care Financing Administration (HCFA) within the Department of

Health and Human Services (HHS). HCFA delegates the processing of reimbursement claims and initial decisions concerning the coverage of services and certain reimbursement issues to private insurance carriers with which it has contracts for Medicare administration. For Part B (under which most clinical laboratory testing is reimbursed), these insurance companies are called "carriers." For Part A, these insurance companies are called "intermediaries."

Q.2:7 What is the reimbursement method for most clinical laboratory tests performed for Medicare beneficiaries?

Clinical laboratory testing performed for ambulatory patients by hospitals, independent laboratories, and physicians' office laboratories is reimbursed pursuant to Medicare fee schedules. Fee schedules, as the name implies, establish a specific reimbursement level for each individual laboratory test. Fee schedules are established on a locality-by-locality basis by Medicare carriers and first became effective July 1, 1984.

Briefly, fee-schedule reimbursement means that hospital, independent, and physicians' office laboratories performing clinical diagnostic testing receive as payment from Medicare the lowest of the following:

- The laboratory's or the physician's actual charge,
- The applicable fee schedule amount, or
- A "national limitation amount" that is set at a certain percentage of the median of the fee schedules.

For a more detailed discussion of clinical laboratory fee-schedule reimbursement, see L.R.M., Part 9.1, Section 3-2.

Q.2:8 Does the method of Medicare reimbursement vary based on the site of service?

Yes, because the fee-schedule method of reimbursement does not apply to testing performed in certain types of facilities.

Specifically, fee-schedule reimbursement does not apply to clinical laboratory testing in the following categories:

- Tests furnished to a hospital inpatient covered by Part A of Medicare;
- Tests performed for the patients of a skilled nursing facility;
- Tests furnished by an end-stage renal disease (ESRD) facility covered by Medicare rules for ESRD payments;
- Tests provided by hospitals that hold Medicare-granted waivers from fee-schedule reimbursement, or hospitals located in states or regions that have other types of Medicare-granted waivers from general Medicare reimbursement principles;
- Tests provided to patients of certain rural health clinics;
- Tests provided by Medicare-participating health maintenance organizations or similar plans to their enrollees; and
- Tests provided by a hospice.

Thus, independent and physician's office laboratories are generally reimbursed under the fee schedules.

Q.2:9 How does the Common Procedural Terminology (CPT) Code relate to Medicare?

The Common Procedural Terminology (CPT) Code is a publication of the American Medical Association (AMA) that identifies thousands of diagnostic and therapeutic procedures, including clinical laboratory tests, by five-digit codes. These codes are widely used to identify procedures in claims submitted to private and government health insurance programs. The CPT codes form the basis for the coding system for Medicare claims, the HCFA Common Procedural Coding System (HCPCS).

Q.2:10 Do Medicare reimbursement principles treat panel or profile tests differently from other tests?

Yes. The Medicare codes for clinical laboratory testing include a series of codes (80001–80019) that apply to multichannel chemistry panels, as well as other codes that apply to various organ disease-related panels. Medicare reimbursement principles provide that, when such panels are billed, the panel code must be used, rather than the codes for individual test components of the panel, and the reimbursement level established for the panel code will apply. [See *Medicare Carriers Manual* §5114.1.L.]

Q.2:11 Are there any recent, significant examples of the enforcement of panel reimbursement principles?

Yes. On May 5, 1993, HCFA issued a "National Medicare Fraud Alert" concerning an allegedly fraudulent billing practice for profiles based on panel tests. All Medicare carriers were to distribute this alert. The document described the allegedly fraudulent practice as follows:

> A large, interstate, clinical laboratory recently entered into a settlement with a U.S. Attorney to repay more than $110 million to the Medicare and Medicaid programs for submitting false claims and pleaded guilty to criminal charges. The scheme resulted in physicians ordering medically unnecessary services, and involved Sequential Multi-Analysis Computer (SMAC) (For the years 1987–1992, CPT codes 80002–80019 are applicable), HDL-cholesterol test procedure code 83718, LDL test procedure code 83720 (lipid profile 80061, total cholesterol 82465), and serum ferritin tests (82728).
>
> The scheme was a [sic] follows. When a physician ordered SMAC, the laboratory would also perform, and bill the physician a nominal amount for, the HDL-cholesterol test. If the physician objected, the additional charge would be dropped. New physician clients were told the test was free. The laboratory did not inform the physicians that it was billing insurers, such as Medicare, for the test ($18 for SMAC, $16 for HDL-cholesterol). The laboratory subsequently revised its pre-printed test ordering

> form, changing the item, SMAC, to Health Survey Profile. Health Survey Profile consisted of both SMAC and the HDL-cholesterol test. Thus, whether the HDL-cholesterol test was medically necessary or not, the physician was induced to order it.
>
> Subsequently, the laboratory added the serum ferritin test to its Health Survey Profile (at an additional charge to insurers of $16). Again there was a nominal additional charge to physician clients that was waived if the physician objected.
>
> In 1988, Medicare paid the laboratory about $500,000 exclusively for the serum ferritin test. By 1990, Medicare was paying the laboratory $31 million exclusively for the ferritin test. [Health Care Financing Administration, *National Medicare Fraud Alert* (May 5, 1993)]

Q.2:12 How does the Medicare reimbursement system provide payment for specimen collection or trip fees?

Medicare pays a "specimen collection fee" of up to $3 to the party (e.g., the laboratory or the physician) that has actually collected the specimen from the patient. Only one specimen collection fee is allowed per patient encounter, regardless of the number of specimens drawn. The types of specimen collection for which the fee is payable are venipuncture and urine sample collection by catheterization.

There are certain limitations that apply to specimen collection fees. Physicians may receive a specimen collection fee only when it is the accepted and prevailing practice of physicians in the locality, and the particular physician performing the service, to make separate charges for specimen collection. Specimen collection fees are expressly disallowed when the cost of specimen collection is minimal, such as throat cultures, routine capillary punctures for clotting or bleeding time, or stool specimen collection for an occult blood test. Similarly, routine handling charges when a specimen is referred from one laboratory to another are disallowed.

Medicare will also pay specimen collection fees to laboratories when they provide personnel to collect specimens from nursing home and home-bound patients, if it is medically necessary for the specimen to be drawn from the patient, and the laboratory's technician personally draws the specimen. When a technician must travel to a nursing home or patient's home to collect a specimen, travel fees may be paid, but only if the technician actually draws the specimen and does not merely serve as a courier.

Q.2:13 What has been the trend in the level of Medicare reimbursement for laboratory tests during the last ten years?

Since July 1, 1984, when Medicare fee schedules first became effective for clinical laboratories, Medicare fee-schedule reimbursement for laboratories has been steadily reduced in a series of federal budget laws that have cut the level of the "national limitation amount" cap on fee schedule payments. The cap has dropped from its initial level of 115% of the median of local fee schedules (effective July 1, 1986-April 1, 1988), to 100% (effective April 1, 1988–January 1, 1990), to 93% (effective January 1, 1990–January 1, 1991), to 88% (effective January 1, 1991–January 1, 1994). The median cap will continue to drop 4% each year in 1994, 1995, and 1996, reaching a level of 76% of the medians of the fee schedules by January 1, 1996.

Q.2:14 What is "assignment" and how does it relate to clinical laboratories?

Assignment, or *assignment of benefits*, is a Medicare term referring to a provider's agreement to accept the benefits that would otherwise be paid to the patient as reimbursement for services provided to a Medicare beneficiary. Clinical laboratories are subject to a requirement of mandatory assignment in the Medicare law. [42 U.S.C. §1395l(h)(5)(C)] This means that laboratories must agree to accept Medicare's payment as payment in full for the services they provide and bill the Medicare program directly for those services. If a clinical laboratory or other provider of laboratory services does not accept assignment for laboratory testing, Medicare will not pay for it.

Q.2:15 Who gets billed when laboratories perform tests for Medicare beneficiaries?

Medicare's assignment provisions require clinical laboratories to bill the Medicare program directly for the fee-schedule testing they perform. Exemptions from the direct billing requirement exist for certain laboratory-to-laboratory referrals that meet specific conditions identified in the Medicare law.

Specifically, Medicare need not be billed directly in the case of a laboratory-to-laboratory referral if any of the following conditions is met:

- Either of the two referring laboratories is a wholly owned subsidiary of the other;
- Both laboratories are wholly owned subsidiaries of a third;
- The referring laboratory is located in or is part of a rural hospital; or
- No greater than 30% of the tests for which a referring laboratory receives requisitions in a year are performed by another laboratory. [42 U.S.C. §1395l(h)(5)(A)]

Q.2:16 How are hospital laboratories reimbursed by Medicare?

For testing performed on ambulatory patients by hospital laboratories, Medicare reimbursement is the fee-schedule reimbursement described above. In the case of hospital inpatients, the laboratory is reimbursed as part of the hospital. Hospitals that participate in the Medicare program are generally reimbursed under the Prospective Payment System (PPS), in which the diagnosis-related group (DRG) is the basic unit of payment. Payment is made per

DRG, and the DRG method adjusts payments to compensate for the severity of each hospital's case mix and certain other factors.

Some hospitals are exempt from the PPS system and are paid on the basis of their reasonable costs of operation. Hospital outpatient services, including laboratory tests provided to outpatients, are paid on a reasonable cost basis.

For a more extended discussion of hospital reimbursement, see L.R.M., Part 9.1, Sections 3-3 and 4.

Q.2:17 Does Medicare provide for any appeals process when reimbursement is reduced or denied?

Yes. If a provider or supplier disagrees with a reimbursement decision by Medicare, the provider or supplier may avail itself of the Medicare appeals process. In broad terms, Medicare payment appeals pass through the same general stages whether Part A or Part B is involved. The first stage is a reconsideration by the carrier or intermediary (the insurance company to which the federal government delegates authority for processing Medicare claims). If a decision in this reconsideration is unfavorable to the provider, the provider may have an administrative hearing by HHS, further administrative review, and in some instances, judicial review. The appeals process varies somewhat depending on whether Part A or Part B is involved. For a more detailed discussion of the Medicare appeals process, see L.R.M., Part 9.1, Section 7.

Q.2:18 Can the Medicare program recover payments from laboratories when authorities think too much has been paid?

Yes. The Medicare statute and regulations provide that Medicare carriers and intermediaries can recover "overpayments" if reimbursement was too high or if the services provided were later determined to be not "reasonable and necessary" for diagnosis or treatment. When a carrier or intermediary attempts to recover such overpayments, it can offset overpayments against payments due under outstanding claims. Any decision by the carrier or intermediary to seek recovery of overpayments is subject to the appeals process.

Q.2:19 What sanctions apply to laboratories in connection with the Medicare program?

A variety of sanctions can apply to clinical laboratories and other suppliers of services to Medicare beneficiaries. For example, a laboratory can be subjected to financial civil penalties for submitting false or fraudulent claims, and can be subject to exclusion from participation in Medicare or Medicaid, and/or fines and/or imprisonment of officers or directors, for similar conduct. [See 42 U.S.C. §§1320a-7, 1320a-7(a), 1320a-7b(a).] A laboratory may also be subject to criminal sanctions for a wide range of activities that are defined by statute as "kickbacks, bribes or rebates." [42 U.S.C. §1320a-7b(b)] Additionally, a Medicare law prohibits the submission of claims for laboratory services to Medicare when "self-referral" occurred; that is, the referral for the testing was made by a physician who had a statutorily defined ownership or compensation relationship with the clinical laboratory. [42 U.S.C. §1395nn]

The subject of potential clinical laboratory fraud and abuse is extensive and complex. For a more detailed discussion, see Chapter 4; see also, L.R.M., Part 7.1 and Part 9.1, Sections 8 and 10.

3

State Licensure of Clinical Laboratories

Q.3:1 Which states require clinical laboratory licensure?

The following require clinical laboratory licensure for some or all of the laboratories operating within their borders:

- Alabama
- Alaska
- Arizona
- Arkansas
- California
- Colorado
- Connecticut
- Delaware
- Florida
- Georgia
- Hawaii
- Idaho
- Illinois
- Indiana
- Kansas
- Kentucky
- Maine
- Maryland
- Massachusetts
- Michigan
- Minnesota
- Mississippi
- Montana
- Nebraska
- Nevada
- New Mexico
- New York
- New York City
- North Carolina
- North Dakota
- Ohio
- Oklahoma
- Oregon
- Pennsylvania
- Rhode Island
- South Dakota
- Tennessee
- Texas
- Utah
- Vermont
- Virginia
- Washington
- West Virginia
- Wisconsin
- Wyoming

However, it should be noted that some of these states' licensure requirements apply only to hospitals (and thus, hospital laboratories); other licensure programs apply only to laboratories performing particular tests in certain areas, typically premarital syphilis and rubella testing or testing for the human immunodeficiency virus (HIV).

Q.3:2 How do state licensure requirements relate to CLIA'88?

The state clinical laboratory and hospital licensure requirements are independent of the federal law requirements contained in CLIA'88. CLIA'88 provides that no state is to be prevented from taking any action or enforcing any laws to the extent that such laws are not inconsistent with CLIA'88 or its implementing regulations. Additionally, if a state enacts laboratory laws that are equal to or are more stringent than CLIA'88 and its implementing regulations, the Department of Health and Human Services (HHS) may exempt laboratories in that state from the requirement to comply with CLIA'88 requirements.

Q.3:3 How do state licensure requirements relate to Medicare?

Medicare is a federal program of health insurance, whereas state licensure requirements for hospitals and clinical laboratories generally prescribe the performance standards that such entities must meet in order to operate in the state or provide services to residents of the state.

Q.3:4 How are state laboratory licensure programs administered?

Typically, the state clinical laboratory licensure programs are administered by the state department of health, department of public welfare, or similar entity, and by a specialized unit within the department that is specifically responsible for clinical laboratory licensure and regulation.

Q.3:5 Do state licensure requirements vary by site of service?

In many states, laboratory licensure requirements vary by site of service, either because licensure requirements apply only to hospitals or because physicians' office laboratories are exempt from licensure requirements, or both.

Q.3:6 What aspects of laboratory performance are covered by state licensure requirements?

Those states that require licensure for clinical laboratories usually have standards relating to personnel, proficiency testing, the adequacy of facilities, equipment and materials, and quality control. A few states, such as Georgia, require specific licenses for certain laboratory personnel.

Q.3:7 What are some examples of state licensure requirements?

Two examples of state licensure requirements are Alabama and Florida, both of which have recently updated their requirements. These states' laboratory licensure requirements are as follows.

ALABAMA

An independent clinical laboratory may be issued either a regular license or a temporary license by the Alabama State Board of Health. The temporary license indicates a degree of noncompliance with the State's clinical laboratory rules. It may be issued when the Board is satisfied that steps to achieve compliance are being taken, and the health and safety of patients and personnel are not being endangered by the noncompliance.

A separate license is required for each independent laboratory when more than one laboratory is subject to common management or control.

The fee for any type of clinical laboratory license is $100. This fee must be paid at the time the laboratory applies for the license. Alabama clinical laboratory licenses last for one year and expire on December 31 of the year in which they are granted. The laboratory must reapply for a license and pay the $100 fee annually.

Alabama's laboratory license requirements include specific standards for personnel. The **director** must meet one of the following standards:

- Be a licensed practitioner of the healing arts with at least two years of pertinent laboratory experience; or
- Hold an earned doctoral degree from an accredited institution with a chemical, physical, or biological science as his or her major subject, and be certified by the American Board of Medical Microbiology, American Board of Clinical Chemistry, or other national accrediting board with equivalent standards accepted by the state health department in whatever laboratory specialty or specialties he or she directs; or
- Have four or more years of general clinical laboratory training and experience, of which at least two years must have been spent acquiring proficiency in a laboratory specialty in the laboratory of a hospital, health department, university or medical research institution, or laboratory providing equivalent training that is accepted by the Alabama Department of Health, with the training occurring under a doctoral-level director.

The **supervisor** must meet one of the following requirements:

- Be a licensed practitioner of the healing arts with at least two years of pertinent laboratory experience; or
- Have earned a doctoral degree from an accredited institution with a chemical, physical, or biological science as a major subject and have at least two years' experience in one of the laboratory specialties in the laboratory of a hospital, health department, university or medical research institution, or laboratory providing equivalent training that is accepted by the Alabama Department of Public Health; or

- Have a master's degree from an accredited institution with a major in one of the chemical, physical, or biological sciences and have at least four years of pertinent laboratory experience in which not less than two years have been spent working in one of the laboratory specialties in the clinical laboratory of a hospital, health department, university or medical research institution, or in a clinical laboratory providing equivalent training that is accepted by the Alabama Department of Public Health; or
- Hold a bachelor's degree from an accredited institution with a major in one of the chemical, physical, or biological sciences and have at least six years of pertinent laboratory experience of which not less than two years have been spent working in one of the laboratory specialties in the laboratory of a hospital, health department, university or medical research institution, or clinical laboratory providing equivalent training and accepted by the Alabama Department of Public Health; or
- Have successfully completed three years of academic study in an accredited college or university with a chemical, physical, or biological science as a major subject; meet the requirements for a technologist under the Alabama laboratory rules; and have six years of experience in the laboratory of a hospital, health department, university or medical research institution, or laboratory providing equivalent training and accepted by the Alabama Department of Public Health; or
- Have achieved a satisfactory grade on a proficiency examination for technologist approved by the federal HHS and have six years of full-time laboratory experience obtained after passing the proficiency exam.

There are certain exceptions to these requirements for emergency situations.

A **technologist** must meet one of the following requirements:

- Have successfully completed a full course of study meeting the academic requirements for a bachelor's degree in medical technology from an accredited college or university; or

- Have successfully completed three years of academic study in an accredited college or university and a course of training of at least 12 months in a school of medical technology approved by the Council on Medical Education and Hospitals of the American Medical Association; or
- Have successfully completed a course of study in an accredited college or university that meets all academic requirements for a bachelor's degree in one of the chemical, physical, or biological sciences and have completed at least one year of pertinent laboratory experience in the specialties or subspecialties in which he or she performs tasks, provided that this combination of study and training has given the individual the equivalent in the pertinent specialties or subspecialties of the education and training described in the two items above; or
- Have successfully completed three years of academic study in an accredited college or university with a chemical, physical, or biological science as a major subject and at least one year of experience in the laboratory of a hospital, health department, university or medical research institution, or clinical laboratory providing equivalent training and accepted by the Alabama Department of Public Health; or
- Have achieved a satisfactory grade on a proficiency exam approved by HHS.

The **technician** must meet one of the following requirements:

- Have successfully completed two years of academic study in an accredited college or university and hold an associate's degree in medical technology; or
- Have graduated from high school and subsequently obtained two years of experience as a technician trainee in the clinical laboratory of a hospital, health department, university or medical research institution, or clinical laboratory providing equivalent training and accepted by the Alabama Department of Public Health; or

- Have graduated from high school and successfully completed an official military laboratory procedures course of at least 12 calendar months and obtained at least one year's experience as a technician trainee in the clinical laboratory of a hospital, health department, university or medical research institution, or clinical laboratory providing equivalent training and accepted by the Alabama Department of Public Health.

The Alabama rules provide that no laboratory technician may perform procedures in the absence of a qualified technologist, supervisor, or director.

The **technician trainee** must be a high-school graduate or equivalent who is gaining the required two years of clinical laboratory experience to qualify as a technician, and is participating in a structured training program approved by the State Health Department and designed to provide the trainee with training in a broad range of laboratory procedures of progressive technical difficulties. Technician trainees may perform only repetitive procedures that require a minimal exercise of independent judgment and may perform such procedures only under the personal and direct supervision of a qualified supervisor or technologist.

The Alabama rules contain specific requirements for cytology personnel (cytotechnologist and cytotechnologist supervisor).

With regard to management, the laboratory must be under the direction of a laboratory director and must have enough other qualified personnel to fit the volume and type of tests performed. The laboratory may perform only those procedures that are within the specialties or subspecialties in which the laboratory personnel are qualified. However, the laboratory may perform tests in all specialties if the director or supervisor is a pathologist certified, or eligible for certification, in anatomical and clinical pathology by the American Board of Pathology or American Osteopathic Board of Pathology. The regulations include criteria to establish the qualifications of laboratory personnel in the particular specialties of microbiology, serology, hematology, immunohematology, chemistry, histopathology, and cytotechnology.

With regard to equipment, the laboratory must provide and maintain equipment necessary for the proper performance of the specialties and volume of tests offered. It must comply with all state and local laws and regulations, including those relating to construction and sanitary conditions. All equipment must be in good working order and routinely checked and calibrated. Documentation of these checks and calibrations must be maintained by the laboratory.

Syringes and sharps that are capable of transmitting infection from one person to another must be cleaned and sterilized before each use. Each sterilizing cycle must contain an indicator device that ensures proper sterilization.

There must be quality control procedures in effect, including the use of reference and control sera and other biological samples, calibrating standards, and control charts.

All technical procedures used in the laboratory must be the standard procedures generally accepted by the leading authorities in the specialties identified above or equivalents approved by the Alabama Department of Public Health. The laboratory must maintain notebooks or manuals containing its current testing methods.

With regard to specimen procedures, a specimen may not be tested or reported if one of the following conditions exists:

- Its apparent condition shows that it is unsatisfactory for testing or inappropriate for the test requested;
- It has been collected, labeled, preserved, or otherwise handled in such a manner that it has become unsatisfactory or unreliable as a test specimen; or
- It is perishable and the time lapse between the collection of the specimen and its receipt is so long that the test finding may no longer be reliable.

When a specimen is not tested for any of the above reasons, the laboratory must promptly notify the sender of the specimen and explain why it is not being tested.

The laboratory must report to the Alabama Department of Public Health annually any changes in personnel and any changes in facilities or services affecting the operation of the laboratory.

Laboratories must participate in one or more of the proficiency-testing programs approved by the Alabama Department of Public

Health, and must provide proficiency-testing results to the department for review upon request.

The regulations include requirements for reports on specimens and reports of test results. Specimen reports must contain an identification number, identification of the patient from whom the specimen was taken, the name and address of the practitioner or laboratory submitting the specimen, the date of collection, the condition of unsatisfactory specimens at the time received, the date of receipt, the date of testing, the type of test performed, information concerning the referral of a specimen to another laboratory, the result of the test, and the date the result is reported.

As to reports, duplicate copies of laboratory reports must be filed in the laboratory or stored in a readily accessible location for at least two years. Records and reports of laboratory tests must be treated as confidential information. Tissue pathology reports utilizing acceptable terminology of a recognized system of disease nomenclature must be maintained. Generally, the laboratory director is considered responsible for test reports.

With regard to the building and physical plant of the laboratory, its location and construction must comply with all local building and fire ordinances, and if at all possible, its water must be obtained from a public water supply. Housekeeping facilities and services must be maintained to ensure comfortable and sanitary conditions, the physical plant must be kept in a good state of repair, and safety must be the primary consideration. Temperatures must be maintained so as to provide comfortable working conditions and be appropriate to the procedures being performed. A telephone and extension must be provided to ensure internal and external communication. There must be at least two exits remote from each other leading directly to the outside or to an unobstructed passageway to the outside. Exit doors must be able to accommodate wheelchairs and must open in the direction of exit.

The laboratory must have a properly designed waste disposal system connecting to all fixtures that supply water under pressure. Fire extinguishers and personal safety devices must be provided, and there must be a conspicuously posted fire plan with at least semiannual fire drills. Sufficient lighting must be provided in keeping with requirements for particular tests, and each exit must have an illuminated exit light and direction sign.

Flammable materials, reagents, and gases must be stored in ordinance with requirements of the National Fire Protection Association.

The Alabama rules contain particular requirements for plasmapheresis and whole-blood donor centers and for collection stations.

If a laboratory is out of compliance with any of the applicable licensure provisions, the state board of health may either make the laboratory's licensure status "probational" (provided the health and safety of patients and personnel will not be endangered) or may suspend or revoke the license. The state may also suspend or revoke the license for permitting, aiding, or abetting the commission of any illegal act or for any conduct or practices that the state board of health considers detrimental to the welfare of patients.

Any administrative decision concerning a laboratory licensure is subject to a hearing at which the licensee may present whatever evidence he or she considers necessary and relevant. The hearing is held before the state licensure advisory board, but final decisions as to licensure matters are made by the state board of health. Final decisions on licensure suspension or revocation are subject to judicial review.

FLORIDA

The Florida clinical laboratory licensure law was amended in 1993 and now provides as follows.

Clinical laboratories in the state of Florida are subject to licensure by the state. Exempt from the licensure requirements are the following:

- Clinical laboratories operated by the United States government,
- Clinical laboratories operated and maintained exclusively for research and teaching purposes that do not involve patient or public health service, and

- Clinical laboratories that perform only those tests that are defined as "waived" (pursuant to the CLIA'88 definition of "waived" tests) and that have accordingly been granted a certificate of exemption by the state.

The state Agency for Healthcare Administration (Agency) must promulgate standards for laboratory licensure and performance that comply with the federal CLIA'88 (see Chapter 1) and its implementing regulations for comprehensive quality assurance.

The Agency must promulgate proficiency-testing requirements, including criteria for satisfactory performance on proficiency-testing exams, and may require clinical laboratory personnel to analyze test samples and report on the results of such analyses within a proficiency-testing program.

With regard to clinical laboratory specimens, the statute requires that each specimen must be sent to a laboratory as quickly as possible, but no later than 12 hours after collection, except that this 12-hour requirement does not apply to blood banks or plasmapheresis centers. The specimens may be sent to out-of-state laboratories that hold current licenses issued by the Agency. In the case of referrals to any other laboratory, the test report must state that the testing was done by a reference laboratory and must identify the name and address of that laboratory.

With regard to the laboratory physical plant, the clinical laboratory must comply with all applicable local, county, state, and federal standards for construction and repair. The Agency must establish standards concerning safety and sanitary conditions within a clinical laboratory and its surroundings, including standards for water supply; sewage; specimen handling; identification, segregation, and separation of biohazardous waste; sewage chemicals; work stations; fire safety; and general measures to protect the public health. The Agency must also establish minimum standards for laboratory equipment, its operation, its calibration, and its adequacy for testing procedures.

Each clinical laboratory in Florida must adopt and maintain a written policies and procedures manual that must address items specified in the statute. The manual must be readily available to laboratory personnel and must be followed by them.

The Agency must adopt standards for patient test management, record retention, and test reports. The Agency must also adopt criteria for "alternate site testing" to be performed under the supervision of a clinical laboratory director. ("Alternate site testing" means testing performed under the administrative control of a hospital but performed outside of the physical or administrative confines of the central laboratory.)

The Agency must conduct inspections of each laboratory, collection station, and branch office at least every two years to evaluate compliance with the standards and the statute and regulations to be promulgated thereunder. The inspections may be announced or unannounced. Inspections conducted by private accrediting organizations can be accepted by the Agency in lieu of its own inspections.

An application for a Florida clinical laboratory license must be made by the owner or operator on forms provided by the Agency. A separate license is required of all laboratories maintained on separate premises but under common management. The license will permit the laboratory to perform only those specialties and subspecialties that are within the competence of the laboratory personnel.

Florida laboratory licenses must be renewed biannually. The biannual fees range from $400 for a laboratory performing 2,000 or fewer tests per year to $3,919 for a laboratory performing more than one million tests per year. The biannual fee for a certificate of exemption or a facility surveyed by an approved accrediting organization is $100. However, the licensure fees will not be assessed until the Agency is granted state exemption status under CLIA'88. Until that time, the biannual license fee for all laboratories, regardless of the volume of tests performed, will be $100.

With regard to test requests and results reports, the Florida statute provides that clinical laboratory testing may be performed only at the request of a licensed practitioner, and test results must be reported directly to that person.

The Florida statute specifies grounds for disciplinary action under the licensure provisions and sanctions for such action. The grounds for sanctions include the following:

- Having fraudulent statements on license applications or other documents required by the Agency;
- Allowing unauthorized persons to perform tests or issue reports;
- Having incompetence in testing or reporting;
- Issuing laboratory reports to persons not authorized to receive them;
- Failing to file required reports;
- Reporting test results for specimens on which no tests were performed;
- Testing in a specialty in which the laboratory is not licensed;
- Knowingly advertising false services or credentials;
- Knowingly having a professional connection with, or lending the name of a license laboratory to, an unauthorized laboratory;
- Violating any of the requirements of the statute or the Agency regulations promulgated thereunder, or aiding or abetting such violations;
- Failing to correct deficiencies within the time set by the Agency.

The sanctions for such violations include suspension, revocation, or limitation of a license and administrative fines up to $1,000 per violation. Each day of violation will be subject to a separate fine.

When any condition in a licensed facility presents a clear and present danger to the public health and safety, the Agency may issue an emergency order immediately suspending, revoking, or limiting a laboratory license. The Agency may also bring an injunction to restrain the operation of an unlicensed laboratory or other violation of the statutory requirements and the implementing regulations.

The statute also specifies certain criminal actions by laboratories that will be treated as misdemeanors:

- Operating, maintaining, or directing a clinical laboratory without a license;

- Operating a clinical laboratory that is not under the direction of a licensed laboratory director;
- Allowing any person other than licensed laboratory personnel to perform clinical laboratory procedures except in exempt laboratories; or
- Violating or aiding or abetting in the violation of any provision of the statute or rules promulgated thereunder.

The Florida statute includes specific provisions for the licensure of laboratory personnel.

Laboratories should be aware that the state of Florida has special requirements for laboratories that perform drug testing.

For a detailed review of the laboratory licensure requirements of each state, see L.R.M., Part 5.1.

Q.3:8 Do most states charge fees for clinical laboratory licenses?

Yes. The fees that states charge for clinical laboratory licensure are generally necessary to finance the administration of the licensure requirements.

Q.3:9 What is the range of the fees?

In most states, the fees for obtaining a clinical laboratory license range from $100 to $500. A few states require separate fees for the licensure of certain laboratory personnel.

For information on the laboratory licensure fees of each state, see L.R.M., Part 5.1.

Q.3:10 How long do state laboratory licenses typically last?

In many states, after the issuance of an initial laboratory or hospital license, the license must be periodically renewed, typically at frequencies of one to three years. In some states, such as Illinois, the state licensure agency simply conducts a periodic inspection to verify that the laboratory remains in compliance with state requirements. For detail on licensure periods of each state, see L.R.M., Part 5.1.

Q.3:11 What types of sanctions are typically imposed for violating state laboratory licensure requirements?

In most states, laboratories that fail to comply with licensure requirements may be subject to fines and/or licensure revocation or suspension.

4

Fraud and Abuse

Q.4:1 What types of activities are considered as fraud and abuse?

Generally, the activities that are treated as fraud and abuse incorporate false claims, patient abuse, and a wide variety of activities and business practices that are treated as kickbacks, bribes, or rebates.

Q.4:2 Are fraud and abuse regulated or subject to sanctions at the state or federal level?

Both. Federal laws and an increasing number of state laws establish prohibitions and sanctions for activities that are defined as fraud and abuse.

Q.4:3 What are false claims?

Simply put, the term *false claims* means lying and stealing in the process of making claims to insurers — obtaining money from insurers to which one is not entitled. Some examples of "false claims," drawn from the Medicare program's false claims prohibition, include the following:

- Submitting an accurate claim, but providing false information to support it;

- Concealing information, or failing to disclose it, regarding the right of a patient to benefits;
- Obtaining benefits that are due solely to another provider or a beneficiary;
- Submitting a claim for physician's services that were provided by an unlicensed physician or a nonphysician practitioner;
- Billing for services that were not provided;
- Billing for services that were not medically necessary;
- Billing for services that were unsuitable for the patient's needs or of substandard quality;
- Committing flagrant and persistent overutilization;
- Billing for uncovered services disguised as covered services (e.g., billing for an uncovered laboratory test as a covered test);
- Misrepresenting dates and descriptions of the services rendered, of the identity of the recipient, or of the individual who rendered the service;
- Presenting duplicate billing, including the submission of two claims for the same service or the submission of a claim to the insurer and a claim to the beneficiary for the same service;
- Billing for services that differ from those that were actually performed;
- Presenting claims for services performed by an unlicensed person practicing medicine;
- Presenting claims for services provided by persons or entities that have been excluded from participating in Medicare or Medicaid;
- Entering into arrangements, such as the payment of commissions or the splitting of fees, that result in overcharging;
- Failing to refund payment received from a beneficiary by a physician who declines assignment for medically unnecessary services;
- Violating an assignment agreement;
- Violating a participation agreement by billing a beneficiary rather than the program;
- Violating limiting charge provisions;

- Failing to make the necessary disclosures or obtain the required approvals prior to elective surgery; and
- Maintaining higher schedules of charges for Medicare patients than for other patients.

Q.4:4 What are kickbacks, bribes, and rebates?

The term *kickbacks, bribes, and rebates* is found in a Medicare/Medicaid statutory prohibition on those activities at 42 U.S.C. §1320a-7b(b). Because the Medicare/Medicaid definition of this term has been adopted in identical or similar form in many state laws, it can be viewed as the model for the definition of *kickbacks, bribes, and rebates* generally.

The Medicare prohibition broadly defines the term *kickbacks, bribes, and rebates* to encompass the offer, request, or receipt of payments or other remuneration, directly or indirectly, overtly or covertly, in cash or in kind, to induce referrals for medical services (in the Medicare/Medicaid context, services that are reimbursable by those programs).

The Medicare/Medicaid statutory prohibition includes exceptions for the following:

- Payments that are discounts reported and passed on to the programs;
- Employee reimbursement payments;
- Payments in certain group-purchasing arrangements; or
- Payments that are permitted by federal regulations.

You should be aware of a landmark case that established a broad interpretation of the antirebate law in the mid-1980s. In *United States v. Greber*, 760 F.2d 68 (3rd Cir. 1985), a federal court of appeals interpreted the antiinducement language of the statute. The case involved a physician who was president of a company that provided physicians with diagnostic services. The company billed Medicare for the services and fowarded a portion of the payment to the referring physician.

The government contended that the payments to referring physicians constituted illegal remuneration in violation of the rebate prohibition. Dr. Greber maintained that the payments were interpretation fees for the referring physicians' initial consultations and for their subsequent explanations of test results. He also argued that, absent a showing that the sole purpose of the fee was improperly to induce future services, the compensation for services actually rendered could not violate the antirebate provision. The court, however, held that "[i]f the payments were intended to induce the [referring] physician to use [Dr. Greber's] services, the statute was violated, *even if the payments were also intended to compensate for professional services.*" 760 F.2d at 72 (emphasis added). The *Greber* case has thus been cited consistently for the proposition that if an arrangement is intended even *in part* to induce Medicare referrals, it may violate the antirebate law.

Q.4:5 What major federal laws address health care fraud and abuse?

The major federal laws that specifically address health care fraud and abuse are the Medicare/Medicaid fraud and abuse provisions. These laws do the following:

- Prescribe civil monetary penalties and criminal sanctions for broadly defined false claims [see 42 U.S.C. §§1320a-7a and 42 U.S.C. 1320a-7b(a)];
- Establish criminal sanctions for kickbacks, bribes, and rebates [see 42 U.S.C. §1320a-7b(b) and **Q.4:4**, above]; and
- Prescribe exclusion from Medicare/Medicaid for a variety of activities that are defined as abuse of the programs or patients [see 42 U.S.C. §1320a-7.]

Additionally, there are various federal laws that establish sanctions for false claims or fraud against government agencies generally. These laws include the general, federal civil False Claims Act, 31 U.S.C. §3729; the federal criminal false claims statute, 18 U.S.C. §287; and the mail fraud statute, 18 U.S.C. §1341, which broadly prohibits the use of the mail in furtherance of any fraudulent scheme.

Q.4:6 What federal agencies enforce fraud and abuse laws?

A variety of federal agencies are involved in the enforcement of the Medicare/Medicaid fraud and abuse laws. The Department of Health of Human Services (HHS) Office of the Inspector General (**OIG**) has responsibility for initiating actions to exclude providers of services from Medicare/Medicaid or to impose civil money penalties on providers for fraudulent and abusive activities. The OIG has investigation and subpoena authority to support its enforcement responsibilities. The federal **Department of Justice** has responsibility for investigation and prosecution of certain civil wrongs and criminal fraudulent and abusive conduct. In addition, **Medicare carriers and intermediaries and state Medicaid agencies** have units that are responsible for identifying potentially fraudulent conduct and making referrals for further enforcement to the OIG or the Department of Justice. Additionally, the Federal Bureau of Investigation (**FBI**) has authority to investigate potential criminal fraud and abuse.

Q.4:7 What are the "safe harbors"?

The "safe harbors" are federal regulations issued by the OIG to identify and define those types of activities that will be considered **not** subject to prosecution as kickbacks, bribes, or rebates under the Medicare/Medicaid antikickback statute, 42 U.S.C. §1320a-7b(b). Among the activities identified by the safe harbors are the following types of arrangements, all of which must meet narrowly defined conditions specified in the regulations in order to be treated as exempt from prosecution:

- Investments in large, publicly traded companies and certain narrowly defined investments in limited partnerships and joint ventures;
- Certain personal services and management contracts;
- Certain space and equipment rental arrangements;
- Certain warranty arrangements;
- Certain referral services;

- Certain group purchasing arrangements;
- Discounts that are reported to the Medicare and Medicaid programs;
- Employee compensation arrangements;
- Certain sales of physician practices;
- Waivers of beneficiary coinsurance and deductibles;
- Incentives offered to enrollees of managed care plans;
- Negotiated price reduction agreements between managed care plans and health care providers; and
- Certain agreements between hospitals and Medicare Select insurers. [42 C.F.R. §1001.951 *et seq.*]

The OIG emphasizes that these safe harbors are narrowly defined. Thus, before entering into any business arrangement in any of the categories above, a provider of services to the Medicare or Medicaid program should consult the individual safe harbor requirements closely. For a detailed explanation of each safe harbor, see L.R.M., Part 7.1, Section 2-1B4.

Q.4:8 Are there any provisions of the "safe harbors" that address clinical laboratories specifically?

Although none of the safe harbors addresses laboratory services specifically, the OIG discussed the application of the "discount" safe harbor to laboratories at length in the preamble to the safe harbor regulations. There, the OIG said the following:

> [W]e believe that Congress did not intend for this discount exception to apply to price reductions offered to one payor but not to Medicare or Medicaid. For example, we are aware of cases where laboratories offer a discount to physicians who then bill the patient, but do not offer the same discount to the Medicare program. In some of these cases, the discount offered to the physician is explicitly conditioned on the physician's referral of all of his or her laboratory business. Such a 'discount' does not bene-

> fit Medicare, and is therefore inconsistent with the statutory intent for discounts to be reported to the programs with costs and charges reduced appropriately to reflect the discounts.
>
> Another problem exists when an entity, which is both a provider or supplier of items or services and a joint venture partner with referring physicians, makes discounts to the joint venture as a way to share its profits with the physician partners. Very often this entity furnishes items or services to the joint venture and also acts as the joint venture's general partner or provides management services to the joint venture. For example, in some cases a reference laboratory performs testing for another laboratory at a discount price in accordance with a management contract. In other cases, the services the reference laboratory provides are paid on the basis of a percentage of revenues that the joint venture receives from Medicare. These arrangements are not arms length transactions where the joint venture entity shops around for the best price on a good or service.
>
> Rather, it has entered into a collusive arrangement with a particular provider or supplier of items or services that seeks to share its profits with referring physician partners. To clarify that we do not intend to protect these types of transactions which are sometimes made to appear as 'discounts,' we are clarifying the definition of 'discounts' . . . to permit only transactions made on an arms length basis. [56 Fed. Reg. 35,978]

The preamble also discussed the practice of giving away free computers, illustrating with a laboratory example:

> In some cases the computer can only be used as part of a particular service that is being provided, for example, printing out the results of laboratory tests. In this situation, it appears that the computer has no independent

value apart from the service that is being provided and that the purpose of the free computer is not to induce an act prohibited by the statute. Rather, the computer is part of a package of services provided at a price that can be accurately reported to the programs. In contrast, sometimes the computer that is given away is a regular personal computer, which the physician is free to use for a variety of purposes in addition to receiving test results. In that situation, the computer has a definitive value to the physician, and depending on the circumstances, may well constitute an illegal inducement. *[Id.]*

Q.4:9 What sanctions can be imposed on laboratories for fraud and abuse?

Among the sanctions that can be imposed on clinical laboratories for fraudulent and abusive conduct are civil penalties, exclusion or suspension from Medicare/Medicaid, criminal fines, imprisonment of officers and/or directors, and/or injunctions against the continuation of an activity that is deemed to be fraudulent or abusive.

Q.4:10 What are the grounds for exclusion from the Medicare program?

The Medicare/Medicaid exclusion statute, 42 U.S.C. §1320a-7, and implementing regulations at 42 C.F.R. §§1001.1 *et seq.*, prescribe two types of exclusion: (1) **mandatory** and (2) **permissive**.

Mandatory exclusion is required for individuals or entities that have been convicted of certain Medicare- or Medicaid-related crimes.

Permissive exclusion, which may be imposed at the discretion of HHS, can apply to a wide variety of activities, including the following:

- Conviction for an offense relating to fraud, for obstruction of an investigation, for illegal use of a controlled substance, or for state licensure sanctions;

- Excessive charges, unnecessary services, or substandard quality services;
- False claims;
- Activities prohibited by the Medicare/Medicaid antirebate statute (see **Q.4:4**, above);
- Ownership or control by a person who has been convicted of a criminal offense related to Medicare or Medicaid or has had civil money penalties imposed under the Medicare civil money penalties law (see **Q.4:5**, above);
- Failure to disclose, or withholding of, information required to be disclosed to Medicare and Medicaid;
- Failure to grant access to federal authorities for determinations of compliance with regulatory requirements;
- Default on a student loan;
- Violation of a hospital corrective action plan imposed under the prospective payment system;
- Violation of limiting charges under the physicians' fee schedule; and others.

Q.4:11 What are the grounds for exclusion from the Medicaid program?

The grounds for exclusion from the Medicaid program are largely the same as the grounds for exclusion from the Medicare program. [See 42 U.S.C. §1320a-7 and 42 C.F.R. §§1001.1 *et seq*.]

Q.4:12 What is the Stark law?

The Stark law is a federal statute that establishes sanctions, including civil money penalties, for billings to Medicare and Medicaid for clinical laboratory and other "designated health services" by an entity with which the referring physician has an ownership or compensation relationship, as defined in the law. [42 U.S.C. §1395nn] The Stark law is often referred to as a prohibition on "physician self-referral." For a detailed discussion of the Stark self-referral law, see L.R.M., Part 9.1, Section 10.

Q.4:13 What types of services, other than laboratory tests, are covered by the Medicare/Medicaid self-referral restrictions?

In 1993, Congress enacted a law that expanded the coverage of the original Stark self-referral prohibition, which applied only to clinical laboratory services. The expanded law applies to "designated health services." They are defined to include the following:

- Clinical laboratory tests,
- Radiology,
- Physical therapy,
- Occupational therapy,
- Durable medical equipment,
- Prosthetics and orthotics,
- Parenteral and enteral nutrition,
- Inpatient and outpatient hospital services,
- Prescription drugs, and
- Home health services.

The expansion of the self-referral law to these additional services and to services reimbursed by Medicaid as well as Medicare generally becomes effective January 1, 1995.

Q.4:14 Do states also regulate fraud and abuse by clinical laboratories?

Yes. States have independent authority to regulate fraudulent and abusive activity by health care providers of services to state residents.

Q.4:15 What types of state laws address clinical laboratory fraud and abuse?

Some states have enacted statutes that prohibit fraud in connection with the billing or provision of services to the state Medicaid recipients and/or prohibit kickbacks, bribes, or rebates in connection with the provision of services to state Medicaid beneficiaries. Other states, such as California, have adopted prohibitions on kickbacks, bribes, and rebates that apply to all health care services, not just those provided to Medicaid beneficiaries. Many state laws establish penalties or physician disciplinary sanctions for the practice of "fee splitting," which, under some state statutory formulations, can include arrangements between physicians and laboratories that are similar to kickbacks, bribes, and rebates.

Q.4:16 What is an example of a state fee-splitting law?

Kansas' fee-splitting law is an example of those addressed within the context of physician licensure and disciplinary provisions. The Kansas Medical Practice Act includes the following section:

> *Professional incompetency, unprofessional conduct, false advertisement and advertisement, license and licensee defined . . .*
>
> . . . (b) 'Unprofessional conduct' means . . .
>
> . . . (19) Directly or indirectly giving or receiving any fee, commission, rebate or other compensation for professional services not actually or personally rendered, other than through the legal functioning of lawful professional partnerships, corporations or associations. [Kan. Stat. Ann. §65-2837]

This law prohibits not only the giving but also the receipt by a physician of "compensation for professional services not actually or personally rendered."

Q.4:17 Do private insurers have the authority to regulate fraud and abuse?

Private insurers do not have regulatory authority similar to that of the federal or state governments. However, when private insurers have contractual relationships with providers, such as may exist in the case of health maintenance organization (HMO) or preferred provider organization (PPO) arrangements, insurers can include contractual terms that make it a contract violation to engage in fraudulent or abusive activities.

Q.4:18 Can fraud committed against private insurers be prosecuted as a crime?

Yes. Fraudulent activities involving private insurers, such as false claims, can be subject to prosecution under the federal mail fraud law, 18 U.S.C. §1341, when such activities are carried out in some manner that involves the use of the mail—for example, to send claims filings to the insurer. A good example in the context of diagnostic services is the recent case of *United States v. Hooshmand*, 931 F.2d 725 (11th Cir. 1991).

In this case, the defendant physician provided certain diagnostic tests to his own patients and to patients of other physicians. The alleged offense involved billing for consultations as opposed to services for new patients; both Medicare and private insurers paid higher amounts for consultations than new-patient services. Dr. Hooshmand was charged with Medicare fraud under 18 U.S.C. §287 for submitting false "consultation" claims to Medicare and with mail fraud under 18 U.S.C. §1341 for using the mail to submit false "consultation" claims to private insurers. The evidence showed that Dr. Hooshmand submitted claims to both Medicare and private insurers for consultations, when in fact the services were provided to his own patients, and no consultation was requested by anyone else.

One of the issues involved in determining whether the physician had the requisite knowledge for criminal action was whether he knew of the insurers' definitions of the term *consultation* and the fact that consultations were paid at a higher rate. In both cases, the court found evidence of the physician's familiarity with the insurers' manuals sufficient to establish the requisite knowledge. With regard to evidence supporting Dr. Hooshmand's knowledge that his billings to private insurers for consultations were fraudulent, the court acknowledged that the private insurers' manuals defined the term *consultation* as a request for an examination by "a physician or other appropriate source," and that the testimony of other physicians, as well as Dr. Hooshmand's expert on Medicare billing, indicated that the language "other appropriate source" was deemed to include self-referrals by patients, referrals by a patient's neighbor or friends, or even self-referrals from patients selecting a physician from the telephone directory.

The court suggested that such broad interpretations of the term *consultations* were reasonable, and that, had Dr. Hooshmand actually believed and relied on such interpretations, his conduct with respect to the private insurers might not have been fraudulent. The court went on to note, however, that Dr. Hooshmand's staff testified that he had instructed them to address consultation reports to physicians who never requested them and to place copies of these reports in patients' files so that the reports could be used to satisfy *private* insurance claims adjusters looking for documentation of a consultation claim. This evidence, the court indicated, revealed that Dr. Hooshmand interpreted the private insurers' manuals, like the Medicare manual, to require a consultation to rest on a request from another physician, and that Dr. Hooshmand was consciously scheming to create evidence of such requests when none had been made.

Q.4:19 Are there any provisions of medical ethics that address fraud and abuse?

Fraud and abuse involving physicians have traditionally violated the ethics of the medical profession. The *Principles of Medical Ethics* of the American Medical Association (AMA) calls on physicians to be honest and law-abiding. The *Current Opinions of the Council on Ethical and Judicial Affairs* of the AMA (AMA: Chicago 1992) include prohibitions on fee splitting and the provision of unnecessary or "worthless" services.

Q.4:20 Have there been any landmark fraud and abuse cases involving clinical laboratories?

Two landmark fraud and abuse cases involving clinical laboratories occurred during the 1990s. One, the *Hanlester* case, involved the Medicare/Medicaid antirebate law. The other, the *NHL* case, involved false claims allegations based on billings for certain chemistry profiles.

Q.4:21 What happened in the *Hanlester* case?

The *Hanlester* case resulted from a lengthy investigation of some California clinical laboratories by the OIG. The activity prosecuted by the OIG in *Hanlester* was physician limited partnerships furnishing health care services. The defendants were a California general partnership—the Hanlester Network (Hanlester); the corporation that owned a majority interest in Hanlester; various Hanlester principals; and three clinical laboratory limited partnerships formed by the Hanlester Network and its principals. The partnerships were operated under the names PPCL (in Orange County, California), Omni (in the Pasadena, California area), and Placer (in the Sacramento, California area). Not named as a defendant in the case but integrally involved in it was Hanlester's former vice president/marketing. The vice president/marketing was responsible for selling to prospective physician investors limited partnerships in three clinical laboratories.

In 1987 and 1988, the Hanlester Network formed the three limited partnerships, each of which was to own and operate a clinical laboratory in its California locality. In order to solicit investors, Hanlester issued a private placement memorandum offering limited partnership shares in each of the three laboratories. Shares were offered to physicians or entities whose ownership would likely benefit the laboratories. Hanlester did not attempt to recruit nonphysician limited partners.

Regarding the investment, Hanlester made a number of representations in the private placement memorandum issued to prospective partners and in sales presentations. Hanlester represented that initially all business for each laboratory would be obtained from the physician limited partners and, over the life of the partnership, the physician limited partners would continue to be the primary source of partnership business. Hanlester also told prospective limited partners that, although partners were being sought from among physicians who regularly ordered outpatient tests in the relevant geographical areas, some business would be solicited from nonpartner physicians and that patronage of the partnerships' laboratories by the limited partners was voluntary. Hanlester did, however, warn prospective partners that if they purchased shares in the partnerships and did not refer their laboratory testing business to the partnership laboratories, the investments would fail. However, Hanlester stated that returns on investment in the partnerships would not be based on patient referrals from the partners, but rather on the profits earned by the partnerships.

When it came to conducting the business of the three laboratories, Hanlester established a laboratory management services contract with a large nationwide clinical laboratory network, SmithKline BioScience Laboratories, Inc. (SKBL). With respect to the operation of the laboratories, SKBL referred the bulk of the testing to its own facilities.

While the laboratories were in operation, the majority of the tests referred to the partnership laboratories originated from limited partner physicians. In addition, most of the laboratories' revenues came from tests referred by the physician limited partners. Evidence in the case showed that partnership laboratories would not have been profitable unless limited partners referred to them a substantial number of laboratory tests. In 1988 and 1989, the laboratories paid the physician limited partners returns on investment equal to 50 percent or more for each laboratory.

Despite these significant returns on investment, there were problems at the partnership laboratories. Referring physicians experienced problems with the quality of services provided by the laboratories, including failure to pick up laboratory test requests and problems related to billing and collections. As a result, some of the limited partners reduced their referrals to the partnership laboratories. Hanlester became aware of this reduction in referrals because it monitored the usage of the laboratories by the limited partners. Hanlester's operations vice president enlisted the medical director of the partnerships to phone physicians whose referrals to the laboratories had decreased in an effort to enhance referrals by improving the quality of service at the laboratories.

The medical director asked the limited partners to explain why they were not referring more business and advised them that, between their referrals and those of other limited partners, the partners he telephoned were not referring enough business to the laboratories. He pointed out that their failure to refer sufficient business was detrimental to the interests of the laboratories as well as those of the other limited partners.

The OIG argued that Hanlester's limited partnership arrangements violated the antirebate statute's prohibition against knowing and willful offers or payment of any "remuneration" to any person to "induce" that person to refer Medicare patients. The OIG argued that the partnerships constituted unlawful "inducements" because the "investment returns" offered were merely a vehicle through which to channel payments to physicians in order to induce their referrals. The OIG asserted that the arrangement created an illegal inducement even if Hanlester merely established laboratories whose earnings were *dependent*, rather than conditioned, on physician partner referrals; informed prospective partners of that dependency; and strongly *encouraged* partners to refer business to the laboratories.

The core of the defendants' arguments in response was that the antirebate statute should be interpreted as prohibiting only *agreements* to make referrals, and not the mere *encouragement* to make such referrals, so that such arrangements would be unlawful only where becoming a limited partner was *conditioned* upon the referral of business. Defendants contended that a contrary construction would arm the OIG with unbridled discretion to prosecute benign or even procompetitive health care ventures.

A final administrative decision in the case occurred on September 18, 1991. [*Inspector General v. Hanlester Network*, Dkt. Nos. C-186-C-192, C-208, and C-213, Decision No. 1275, HHS Departmental Appeals Board (Sept. 18, 1991)] The Board held that the antirebate statute can be violated when persons or entities knowingly and willfully offer or pay remuneration with the intent of *exercising influence over the reason or judgment* of others in an effort to cause them to refer Medicare or Medicaid business. The Board noted that remuneration offered or paid that exceeds the reasonable value of services provided, or of investment made, is likely intended as inducement for referrals.

The Board further stated that inferences regarding intent may be drawn from the structure of the venture: whether the venture is limited to potential referral sources; whether the partners are precluded or discouraged from using alternative laboratories; whether the investments were sought to meet the capital needs of the venture; and whether the venture met a need for services. It is relevant whether the arrangement was likely to lead physicians to select one laboratory over another or to overutilize laboratory services because of the incentives provided. Evidence showing resulting overutilization or reduced quality of services to recipients/beneficiaries is relevant on whether the incentive offered was sufficient to induce referrals.

The remedy sought by the OIG was exclusion of the defendants from participating in Medicare and Medicaid. The Board said that the appropriateness of exclusion turns on the "trustworthiness" of those against whom the exclusion remedy is sought. Proof of a violation of the statute *alone* suffices to raise an inference of untrustworthiness because the fact that Congress identified specific conduct as grounds for exclusion showed that such conduct was regarded as evidence of untrustworthiness. Once the inference arises, it is the burden of the perpetrator to overcome it or demonstrate mitigating circumstances, not the OIG's burden to establish untrustworthiness.

The Board provided guidance on matters to be considered in evaluating the trustworthiness of the respondents in this case. With respect to the individual respondents, these considerations included the following:

- The circumstances of the misconduct and the seriousness of the offense;
- The degree to which a respondent is willing to place the Medicare and Medicaid programs in jeopardy, even if no actual harm occurs;
- The failure to admit misconduct, show remorse, or demonstrate rehabilitation; and
- The probability that a respondent will commit the same or some similar offense again.

Considering these factors, the Board concluded that all of the corporate and individual respondents should be excluded from the Medicare program. None of the individual respondents had provided sufficient evidence to overcome the inference of untrustworthiness that existed because of their violation of the statute. To the contrary, individual principals of Hanlester were the primary actors in the planning and operation of the partnerships. Accordingly, various periods of exclusion were imposed on the Hanlester respondents.

The *Hanlester* administrative decision was later affirmed in federal court. [(*Hanlester Network v. Sullivan*, [1993-1 Transfer Binder] *Medicare & Medicaid Guide* (CCH) ¶41,076 (C.D. Calif. 1993)] The case represented a substantial victory for the OIG. The case established a broad interpretation of the antirebate statute consistent with the broad interpretations advanced in previous judicial decisions such as *Greber*. (See **Q.4:4**, above.) Moreover, *Hanlester* affirmed the exclusion remedy as a powerful enforcement tool in the hands of the government.

Q.4:22 What happened in the *NHL* case?

The *NHL* case involved a large, interstate clinical laboratory and its packaging of profiles based on sequential multianalysis computer (SMAC) panels with added high-density lipoprotein (HDL)-cholesterol and serum ferritin tests.

The facts were as follows. When a physician ordered an SMAC panel, the laboratory would also perform, and bill the physician a nominal amount for, the HDL-cholesterol test. If the physician objected, the additional charge would be dropped. New physician clients were told the test was free. The laboratory did not inform the physicians that it was billing insurers, such as Medicare, for the test ($18 for SMAC, $16 for HDL-cholesterol). The laboratory subsequently revised its preprinted test-ordering form, changing the item, SMAC, to Health Survey Profile. The Health Survey Profile consisted of both SMAC and the HDL-cholesterol test.

Subsequently, the laboratory added the serum ferritin test to its Health Survey Profile (at an additional charge to insurers of $16).

Again, there was a nominal additional charge to physician clients that was waived if the physician objected.

In 1988, before the addition of the serum ferritin test to the Health Survey Profile, Medicare paid the laboratory about $500,000 exclusively for the serum ferritin test. By 1990, Medicare was paying the laboratory $31 million exclusively for the ferritin test.

These facts were unearthed by the OIG in a lengthy and probing investigation aided by tips from a private "whistleblower" who had been an employee of NHL. Ultimately, the OIG advanced a "false claims" theory that said NHL induced physicians to order medically unnecessary HDL and ferritin tests that NHL billed to Medicare. According to this theory, the tests were unnecessary because physicians were led to believe that Medicare would pay little or no more for the added HDL or ferritin tests, and as a result, the physicians did not consider whether or not these tests were medically necessary when they ordered them.

Ultimately, NHL agreed in 1992 to a $111.4 million settlement in the biggest Medicare fraud case ever. NHL's chief executive officer was sentenced to three months in federal prison, plus halfway-house and supervised-release time, plus a $500,000 personal fine, following a guilty plea.

Q.4:23 What is "whistle blowing"?

Broadly speaking, "whistle blowing" means providing tips to prosecutors that help produce indictments against wrongdoers. Provisions in federal false claims laws called "*qui tam*" permit whistle blowers to initiate cases themselves, then turn the cases over—with key information—to the government for prosecution, and finally to share in government recoveries. These *qui tam* provisions offer whistle blowers—who may be former employees, disgruntled competitors, or anyone else—substantial incentives to volunteer tips and initiate cases. In the *NHL* case (see **Q.4:22**, above), the whistle blower received a $15 million payment out of the government's multimillion-dollar recovery.

5

Clinical Laboratory Billing

Q.5:1 Is clinical laboratory billing regulated at the state or federal level?

Laboratory billing is regulated at both the state and the federal levels. Various state laws address laboratory billing. In addition, the Medicare program requires direct program billing for most clinical laboratory tests, and state Medicaid programs may also impose laboratory billing requirements. There are also provisions that apply to the "factoring" of accounts receivable under Medicare and Medicaid. (See **Q.5:11**, below.)

Q.5:2 What are the different types of billing requirements?

The laboratory billing requirements imposed by state and federal law fall into the following broad categories:

- Truth-in-billing requirements;
- Direct patient billing requirements;
- Provisions requiring various types of test charge disclosures;
- Other provisions affecting charges;
- Billing-related disclosures on test result reports; and
- Antifactoring prohibitions.

Q.5:3 What is a truth-in-billing law?

Truth-in-billing laws require that the bill submitted to the patient–consumer for laboratory charges contains a disclosure of the charges made by the laboratory that actually performed the test. Several truth-in-billing laws also require a separate itemization of the specimen collection and handling charge imposed by the physician or laboratory referring the specimen for test processing.

In some cases, the obligation to make such disclosures falls only on the physician: this is the route taken by statutes in Connecticut, Delaware, Maryland, New Jersey, and Oregon. For example, Oregon's statute, Oreg. Rev. Stat. §676.310, requires a test-ordering physician to prepare a separate, itemized billing showing the charges of other suppliers such as laboratories. Noncompliance subjects the physician to licensing disciplinary action.

In other states, the disclosure responsibility extends beyond the physician. For example, if a laboratory collects the specimen directly from the patient, refers it to another laboratory for testing, reports the test results to the physician, and bills the patient, then the billing–referring laboratory may incur the disclosure obligation. Arizona's truth-in-billing law represents one example of this approach. It provides that the bill to the patient must specify the actual charge by the reference laboratory and the specimen collection charge by the referring laboratory or physician. [Ariz. Rev. Stat. Ann. §36-472.]

Q.5:4 What are some actual examples of truth-in-billing laws?

Three examples of clinical laboratory truth-in-billing laws are those of Connecticut, Delaware, and Texas. They provide as follows:

CONNECTICUT

> Sec. 20-7a. Billing for clinical laboratory services
>
> Any practitioner of the healing arts who agrees with any clinical laboratory, either private or hospital, to make payments to such laboratory for individual tests or test series for patients shall disclose on the bills to patients or third party payors the name of such laboratory, the amount or amounts charged by such laboratory for individual tests

or test series and the amount of his procurement or processing charge, if any, for each test or test series. Any person who violates the provisions of this section shall be fined not more than one hundred dollars. [Conn. Gen. Stat. §20-7a]

DELAWARE

1769. Disclosure of laboratory costs

Any practitioner of the healing arts who bills patients or third party payors for individual tests or test services administered by any private or hospital clinical laboratory shall disclose on the bill the name of such laboratory, the amount or amounts charged by such laboratory for individual tests or test series and the amount of any procurement or processing charge made by such practitioner for each test or test series. If the test is performed at a state laboratory or at any other laboratory at which no charge is made, that fact shall be disclosed by the bill. [24 Del. C. §1769]

TEXAS

161.061. Laboratory Information Required

(a) A person licensed in this state to practice medicine, dentistry, podiatry, veterinary medicine, or chiropractic may not agree with a clinical, bioanalytical, or hospital laboratory to make payments to the laboratory for individual tests, combinations of tests, or test series for a patient unless:

(1) the person discloses on the bill or statement to the patient or to a third party payor the name and address of the laboratory and the net amount paid to or to be paid to the laboratory; or

(2) discloses in writing on request to the patient or third party payor the net amount.

(b) The disclosure permitted by Subsection (a)(2) must show the charge for the laboratory test or test series and may include an explanation, in net dollar amounts or percentages, of the charge from the laboratory, the charge for handling, and an interpretation charge.

161.062. Grounds for License Denial

The agency responsible for licensing and regulating a person subject to this subchapter may, in addition to any other authority granted, deny a license application or other permission to practice if the person violates this subchapter. [Tex. Health & Safety Code §§161.061, 161.062 (1993)]

For other examples of truth-in-billing laws, see L.R.M., Part 7.2, Section 2.

Q.5:5 What is a typical direct patient billing law?

A direct patient billing law, as the name implies, requires the laboratory performing the testing to bill the patient directly for its services. The direct billing law bars physicians from billing patients for laboratory services performed in an outside laboratory. The purpose of such laws, at least in part, is to eliminate markups of charges for clinical laboratory tests by physicians who bill for them.

Q.5:6 What are some actual examples of direct patient billing laws?

New York, Rhode Island, and the Medicare program have all adopted laboratory direct patient billing laws.

NEW YORK

The New York law provides the following:

> §586. Payment for services. 1. It shall be unlawful for any purveyor of clinical laboratory services, directly or indirectly, through any person, firm, corporation or association or its officers or agents, to bill or receive payment, reimbursement, compensation or fee from any person other than the recipient of the services, such recipient being the person upon whom the clinical services have been or will be rendered.
>
> 2. The provisions of subdivision one of this section shall be inapplicable to services rendered by a clinical laboratory operated by the state of New York; and to payment by:
>
> (a) A legal relative of the recipient of the services;
>
> (b) An insurance carrier designated by the recipient of the services;
>
> (c) A hospital as defined in article twenty-eight of this chapter on behalf of an in-patient or out-patient of such hospital having been the recipient of the services;
>
> (d) One purveyor to another purveyor for actual services rendered;
>
> (e) An industrial firm only for its own employees;
>
> (f) A trade union health facility only for its registered patients;
>
> (g) Governmental agencies and/or their specified public or private agent, agency or organization on behalf of the recipient of the services;
>
> (h) A substance abuse program which has been approved to operate by the office of alcoholism and substance abuse services pursuant to the provision of section 23.01 of the mental hygiene law on behalf of clients of such a program having been the recipients of the services; and

(i) A health maintenance organization operating in accordance with article forty-three of the insurance law or article forty-four of this chapter. [New York Public Health Law §586]

RHODE ISLAND

The Rhode Island law provides the following:

23-16.2-5.1. Payment for services rendered by clinical laboratories—Commissions, rebates, and fees—Use of laboratory's name

(a) It shall be unlawful for any purveyor of clinical laboratory services, directly or indirectly, through any person, firm, corporation, or association, or its officers or agents, to bill or receive payment, reimbursement, compensation, or fee from any person other than the recipient of the services, the recipient being the person upon whom the clinical services have been or will be rendered.

(b) The provisions of subsection (a) of this section shall be inapplicable to payment by:

(1) A legal relative of the recipient of the services;

(2) An insurance carrier designated by the recipient of the services;

(3) A hospital on behalf of an in-patient or out-patient of the hospital having been the recipient of the services;

(4) One purveyor to another purveyor for actual services rendered;

(5) An industrial firm only for its own employees;

(6) Governmental agencies and/or their specified public or private agent, agency, or organization on behalf of the recipient of the services.

(c) A clinical laboratory shall not offer or give a commission, rebate or other fee, directly or indirectly, to any person as consideration for the referral of a specimen derived from a human body to a clinical laboratory for examination by the laboratory.

(d) A clinical laboratory shall not solicit or accept a commission, rebate, or other fee, directly or indirectly, from any person as consideration for the referral of a specimen derived from the human body to a clinical laboratory for examination by the laboratory. [R.I. Gen. Laws §23-16.2-5.1]

MEDICARE

The Medicare direct program billing provision applies to assignment-related testing (see Chapter 2) and specifies that Medicare payment may only be made to the laboratory or physician who performed a particular test. The single exception to this direct billing requirement provides that Medicare payments to a referring laboratory for a test performed by a reference laboratory may only occur under the following conditions:

- If either of the two referring laboratories is a wholly owned subsidiary of the other;
- If both entities are wholly owned subsidiaries of a third;
- If the referring laboratory is located in or is part of a rural hospital; or
- If not more than 30% of the tests for which a referring laboratory receives requisitions in a year are performed by another laboratory.

Q.5:7 What types of billing-related disclosure requirements exist?

Some states, in lieu of direct billing requirements, require that a laboratory performing tests notify all patients, including those billed by physicians, of the laboratory's charges for tests performed on their behalf. A Pennsylvania regulation is illustrative: "A notification of all charges for laboratory tests performed for the patient shall be sent to the patient by the clinical laboratory unless the patient has been billed directly or otherwise notified of such charges by the laboratory." [Pa. Clinical Laboratories Rules and Regulations §5.48.]

Other states require billing disclosures about the referring party's charges for collection and forwarding of specimens. Laws of Arizona, Illinois, and Maryland are examples. These provisions require specific itemization of handling, procurement, or processing charges by the referring and billing physician. Illinois' provision is as follows:

> Any person who agrees with any independent or hospital run clinical laboratory to make payments to the laboratory for individual tests or test series for patients shall disclose on the bills to patients of third-party payers the name of the laboratory, the amount or amounts charged by the laboratory for individual tests or test series, and the amount of his procurement or processing charge, if any, for each test or test series. [Ill. Clinical Laboratory Act §7-107.]

For more information on these state laws, see L.R.M., Part 7.2, Sections 4 and 5.

Q.5:8 Do any states require disclosures directly on test-result reports?

Yes. States handle such disclosures in one or more of the following ways.

In some states, when a specimen is referred to an out-of-state laboratory, the test report must bear or be accompanied by a statement that includes the name and address of the laboratory where the findings were obtained.

Some states require that a test report include the name, address, and, in some cases, the director's name of the laboratory performing the examination when it is different from the laboratory accepting the specimen.

In some states, the rendering of a test report on work actually performed at another laboratory without designating the name and address and/or director's name may be a prohibited act that can result in revocation of the laboratory license or criminal penalties.

Q.5:9 Do any states impose limitations on handling charges or markups?

Yes. Some states limit the amount that a physician can charge for specimen handling or the amount that he or she can mark up a laboratory charge when billing the patient. For example, in Arizona, the physician or referring laboratory's specimen collection charge must be "reasonable." [Ariz. Rev. Stat. Ann. §36-472B] Provisions of Florida, Oregon, and Michigan law also include specific limitations on handling charges.

Q.5:10 Do any states directly prohibit physicians from marking up laboratory charges when billing patients?

Yes. California is one example. Its laboratory antimarkup statute provides as follows:

> 655.5. It is unlawful for any person licensed under this division or under any initiative act referred to in this division or for any clinical laboratory to charge, bill, or otherwise solicit payment from any patient, client or customer for any clinical laboratory service not actually rendered by such person or clinical laboratory or under his or her or its direct supervision unless the patient, client, or customer is apprised at the first time of such charge, billing, or solicitation and any subsequent charge, billing, or

solicitation of the name, address, and charges of the clinical laboratory performing the service. The first such written charge, bill, or other solicitation of payment and any subsequent charge, bill, or other solicitation of payment shall separately set forth the name, address, and charges of the clinical laboratory concerned and shall clearly show whether or not such charge is included in the total of the account, bill, or charge.

It is also unlawful for any person licensed under this division or under any initiative act referred to in this division to charge additional charges for any clinical laboratory service that is not actually rendered by the licensee to the patient and itemized in the charge, bill, or other solicitation of payment. This section shall not be construed to prohibit any itemized charge for any service actually rendered to the patient by the licensee. [Emphasis added.]

This section shall not apply to any person or clinical laboratory who or which contracts directly with a health care service plan licensed pursuant to Section 1349 of the Health and Safety Code, if such services are to be provided to members of the plan on a prepaid basis and without additional charge or liability on account thereof.

A violation of this section is a public offense and is punishable upon a first conviction by imprisonment in the county jail for not more than one year, or by imprisonment in the state prison, or by a fine not exceeding ten thousand dollars ($10,000), or by both such imprisonment and fine. A second or subsequent conviction is punishable by imprisonment in the state prison. [CALIF. BUS. & PROFESSIONS CODE §655.5.]

Q.5:11 What billing requirements does the Medicare program impose?

Medicare has a direct billing requirement for clinical laboratory services. (See **Q.5:4**, above.)

The Medicare/Medicaid statutes also include a billing-related provision that prohibits reassignment of claims by physicians and other suppliers of services. [42 U.S.C. §1395u(b)(6)] This provision was intended to stop the practice of "factoring," the use of collection agencies that purchased Medicare or Medicaid receivables at discounted rates and then billed for them in their own names, sometimes submitting incorrect and inflated claims.

The statute provides that no payment for a service provided to an individual under the Medicare program shall be made to anyone other than the individual or the physician or supplier who provided the service, with the following exceptions. Payments may be made to the physician or supplier's employer, if the physician or supplier is required as a condition of employment to turn over fees to the employer; to a facility where a service is provided, if there is a contractual arrangement between the facility and the person providing the service under which the facility submits billing; or under other, very limited circumstances not applicable to clinical laboratory services.

The statute does provide that it is permissible for billing to be performed by an agent of the physician or supplier of services, if such agent is operating pursuant to an agreement under which the agent's compensation is unrelated, directly or indirectly, to the amount of the billings or payments, and the compensation is not dependent on the amounts collected.

The broad antifactoring ban expressed in this statute would apply to clinical laboratories, including independent, hospital, and physician's office laboratories. The statute prohibits laboratories generally from engaging in the practice of "factoring" Medicare or Medicaid accounts, but permits laboratories to hire billing agents to perform billing and collection, as long as such agents' compensation is unrelated to the amount billed to or collected from Medicare or Medicaid or the agent's success in securing collections from these programs.

Q.5:12 What other billing requirements does the Medicaid program impose?

Each state Medicaid program has authority to establish its own requirements for Medicaid-covered services. Most Medicaid state agencies provide suppliers of services to Medicaid beneficiaries a copy of a provider manual or similar document that sets forth Medicaid program requirements, including those related to billing. If you have not received such a document from the Medicaid state agency in your state, it would be a good idea to contact the agency to learn whether there is such a manual and, if so, to obtain a copy of it.

Q.5:13 What requirements are there on "balance billing" of patients for charges not covered by insurance?

Some state and federal provisions limit or prohibit balance billing, the billing to patients of amounts above the amount reimbursed by insurance. For the most part, Medicare prohibits balance billing (i.e., mandates assignment of benefits) for clinical laboratory services. A few states, including Pennsylvania and New York, limit or prohibit balance billing.

Q.5:14 What are the sanctions for violating billing requirements?

Sanctions for violating billing requirements vary from state to state and may be directed at the physician rather than the laboratory. For example, in Arizona, a laboratory that breaks the truth-in-billing law may suffer denial or revocation of its license. [Ariz. Rev. Stat. Ann. §36-473(1)] In Connecticut, a physician who fails to comply with the truth-in-billing law is punishable with a fine of up to $100. [Conn. Gen. Stat. Rev. §20-7a]

In Maryland, by contrast, failure to comply with the truth-in-billing provision is not considered unlawful, but rather is treated as unprofessional conduct, subjecting the physician to potential reprimand, probation, suspension, or even revocation of the right to practice. [Md. Health Occ. Code Ann. §14-504(17).] In some states, however, violation of billing requirements may subject a laboratory or physician to fines and even imprisonment. One example is the New York direct billing law, which provides that a violation is a misdemeanor punishable by imprisonment for up to a year and a fine of up to $500, or both. [N.Y. Public Health Law §586.]

6

Clinical Laboratory Advertising

Q.6:1 What laboratory activities are within the scope of laboratory advertising?

As a general rule, clinical laboratories do not advertise their services to the general public, principally because the decision as to where to send the patients or their specimens for testing is customarily made by the test-ordering physician. Despite the relatively small amount of advertising by laboratories, some states have passed laws designed specifically to control laboratory advertising. Some state prohibitions on advertising prohibit merely false or deceptive representation; others include outright bans on advertising to the general public; still others prohibit only advertising that is aimed at patients, rather than advertising aimed at practitioners.

Q.6:2 Who regulates advertising by clinical laboratories?

Clinical laboratory advertising is regulated directly only by the states. In general, state laws have not distinguished between advertising by independent clinical laboratories, hospital laboratories, or physician's office laboratories. However, laboratory advertising, like all advertising, is subject to the Federal Trade Commission Act, 15 U.S.C. §41 *et seq.*, which protects the public from false and misleading advertising.

Q.6:3 Do advertising laws differentiate between the advertising to the general public and advertising to physicians and other health care practitioners?

Generally, laboratory advertising controls have been designed to eliminate the dissemination of information to persons who are not trained to evaluate it, while still permitting the dissemination of information to trained individuals. Thus, advertisements directed only to physicians, who are trained in medical science and who are usually responsible for the referral of the patient to the laboratory, have been virtually uncontrolled, as long as such advertisements are not deceptive or misleading. Advertising to patients, however, has been controlled, based on the view that members of the lay public lack the medical knowledge necessary to make an informed choice among laboratories.

Q.6:4 What types of controls have states imposed on advertising to the general public?

Several states (including Connecticut, Illinois, Maryland, Massachusetts, New Hampshire, Oregon, Pennsylvania, and Tennessee) have limited or prohibited direct advertising to the general public. For example, the Tennessee law provides that a laboratory's license may be suspended, revoked, or denied for fraudulent advertising for patronage of the general public by means of any advertising medium. [See Tenn. Code Ann. §68-29-126(13).] The recent trend, as noted above, has been for states to restrict only misleading advertising rather than all advertising to the general public. However, it should be noted that New Hampshire has included a general ban on advertising to the general public in its laboratory regulations. [See *New Hampshire Licensure Rules and Regulations—Clinical Laboratories*, §§2030, 2330.]

Some states have prohibited advertisements that imply that a laboratory's license constitutes a state endorsement of its operations. Others, such as Arizona, have required regulatory approval of advertising intended for the general public. Still others, such as Connecticut, Illinois, Oregon, and Pennsylvania, have regulated the size and/or content of signs and/or telephone directory listings.

Q.6:5 What types of controls do states impose on advertising to physicians and health care practitioners?

Despite prohibitions on public advertising, all states appear to permit laboratories to advertise to physicians or medical care facilities. However, some states seek to control the content of advertising to the health care community. For example, Massachusetts allows laboratories to advertise in professional media if the advertising is of an ethical nature and does not contain misleading statements or unsubstantiated claims.

Q.6:6 What types of controls do states impose on advertising with regard to price?

Some states have applied controls to price advertising by health care practitioners through licensure-related restrictions of state laws. One example is California, which regulates all price advertising in the health care field. The California provision applies to the licensed director of a clinical laboratory and to other licensed health care providers and practitioners. It provides that any price advertisement must be "exact," avoiding the use of such phrases as "as low as," "and up," "lowest prices," or words or phrases of similar import. This statute further provides that comparative statements must be based on verifiable data, and that price advertising shall not be fraudulent, deceitful, or misleading; price advertising must clearly identify the price for each product or service; and must specify charges for any related professional services, such as dispensing and fitting. [CALIF. BUS. PROF. CODE §651(c)] California has gone perhaps further than any other state in regulating price advertising in health care.

Q.6:7 What sanctions can be imposed for violating laws relating to clinical laboratory advertising?

Generally, violations of advertising controls constitute grounds for limitation or revocation of a clinical laboratory's state license.

Q.6:8 Which federal laws and agencies regulate clinical laboratory advertising?

Although there is no direct federal regulation of clinical laboratory advertising, advertising by clinical laboratories and all other businesses is subject to the Federal Trade Commission Act, 15 U.S.C. §41 *et seq.*, which prohibits false and misleading advertising. This statute is administered by the Federal Trade Commission (FTC).

Q.6:9 What types of court challenges have there been to the legality of restrictions on clinical laboratory advertising?

Since the mid-1970s, laws on health care advertising, whether imposed by states or municipalities, or self-imposed by professional societies such as the American Medical Association (AMA), have come under strong attack. At the federal level, it has been argued successfully that advertising bans impermissibly encroach on the constitutional guarantee of free speech in the First Amendment.

The FTC has successfully sought to enforce its position that advertising restrictions that are self-imposed by professional societies violate the antitrust laws. One result of these developments is that provisions specifically restricting clinical laboratory advertising have been overturned by federal courts in some cases. Consequently, the validity of similar restrictions is now open to serious question.

In *Virginia State Board of Pharmacy v. The Virginia Citizens Consumer Council, Inc.*, 425 U.S. 748 (1976), the U.S. Supreme Court held that a Virginia statute prohibiting pharmacists from advertising prices of prescription drugs was unconstitutional because truthful, nondeceptive advertising concerning lawful activities falls within the protection of the First Amendment. In *Bates v. State Bar of Arizona*, 433 U.S. 350 (1977), the Supreme Court held unconstitutional a state ban on advertising by lawyers. In *MetPath v. Imperato*, 450 F. Supp. 115 (S.D.N.Y. 1978), the court held New York City's municipal ban on laboratory advertising to be unconstitutional in light of the *Bates* and *Virginia State Board of Pharmacy* cases. Similarly, in *MetPath v. Myers*, 462 F. Supp. 1104 (N.D. Calif. 1978), a California ban on laboratory advertising was held unconstitutional. However, in *Friedman v. Rodgers*, 440 U.S. 1 (1979), the court upheld a Texas ban on the practice of optometry under a trade name. In that case, the court distinguished between a trade name and general advertising on the grounds that trade names can be manipulated by their holders and thus used to deceive the public.

In all of the three cases discussed above concerning advertising bans, the Supreme Court emphasized that some forms of the regulation of advertising, or "commercial speech," are permissible in order to serve significant government interests, provided that they leave open alternative channels to communicate the information disseminated in the advertising.

In the antitrust area, the FTC in October 1979 issued an order requiring the AMA to stop imposing restrictions on advertising, solicitation of patients and contractual practices of its members. The agency stated, however, that the AMA could enforce "reasonable ethical guidelines" governing deceptive advertising, unsubstantiated claims, and solicitation of patients who are especially vulnerable to undue influence. The basis for the agency's order was the view that excessive regulation of advertising could possibly restrict competition in the medical community. A federal appeals court upheld the FTC's decision, and in 1982, the Supreme Court affirmed the federal appeals court's ruling by a tie vote without issuance of an opinion.

7

Medicaid Overview

Q.7:1 What is Medicaid?

Medicaid, a program established by Title XIX of the Social Security Act, is a federal/state cooperative program for the provision of health services to the needy.

Q.7:2 How is the Medicaid program financed?

The Medicaid program is financed by a combination of state and federal funds.

Q.7:3 Who administers the Medicaid program?

Because the federal government provides substantial funding to the states for Medicaid, the states are required to comply with certain federally established prerequisites, and these federal standards are administered by the Health Care Financing Administration (HCFA) of the Department of Health and Human Services (HHS), the same agency that administers the Medicare program.

However, provided that these minimum federal standards are observed, each state is allowed to administer its own Medicaid program. Thus, the direct administration of the Medicaid program in each state is handled by a Medicaid state agency that is typically part of the state's department of health or department of public welfare.

In administering Medicaid, each state participating is required to approach the provision of health care services with the aim of making them readily available to all eligible persons, setting standards to ensure that the services are of high quality. The state must also decide what services it will provide, if any, in addition to those required by the Medicaid statute and the federal regulations.

Q.7:4 How does Medicaid relate to Medicare?

Medicare and Medicaid are separate programs, each supplying funds for the provision of medical services. Medicare is a program of federal insurance for the aged (those over 65) and disabled; Medicaid is a federal/state cooperative program for the provision of medical services to the needy. Because state Medicaid programs must comply with certain federal standards, and the agency that administers Medicare also administers the federal Medicaid requirements, there are many reimbursement policies and principles common to the two programs.

Q.7:5 Who is eligible to receive Medicaid benefits?

Persons eligible to receive Medicaid benefits are low-income persons who are age 65 or over, blind, disabled, or members of families with dependent children or who are qualified pregnant women or children.

Q.7:6 Can a person receive both Medicare and Medicaid benefits?

Yes, because both programs provide health benefits to persons who are over 65. Medicare provides such benefits to all persons over 65, whereas Medicaid provides such benefits to low-income persons who are over 65.

Q.7:7 What are the federal requirements for Medicaid coverage of clinical laboratory tests?

The Medicaid statute contains a requirement that each state's Medicaid plan pay for laboratory services rendered to Medicaid-eligible persons. Thus, the Medicaid statute defines the term *medical assistance* that each state Medicaid program must provide to include "inpatient hospital services," "outpatient hospital services," and "other laboratory . . . services . . . ." [42 U.S.C. §1396d(a)] Federal regulations define *inpatient hospital services* and *outpatient hospital services* in such a way as to include diagnostic laboratory services, and define *other laboratory services* in such a way as to include independent and physician's office laboratory services. [See 42 C.F.R. §§440.10(a), 440.20(a), and 440.30.]

A state Medicaid plan may cover services over and above those that it is required to cover by federal law. Thus, it is possible for a state Medicaid plan to cover a broader scope of laboratory services than the federal coverage standards require. It is not possible to generalize as to which set of laboratory services, if any, are covered by the various state Medicaid plans over and above those that must be covered by federal law. For the specifics of each state Medicaid plan's coverage of laboratory tests, individual state Medicaid agencies must be consulted.

Q.7:8 Are there any particular state requirements for coverage of clinical laboratory tests?

In establishing standards for coverage of services, states must first adhere to federal minimum standards and then may establish their own additional standards. For clinical laboratory services, the federal minimum standards require that, in order to be covered, a test must be required and provided by or under the direction of a physician acting within the scope of his or her practice, and provided by a laboratory that satisfies the requirements of the CLIA'88 regulations. [42 C.F.R. §440.30] Any standards in addition to these federal minimum requirements are established on a state-by-state basis.

Under each state Medicaid plan, there must be a state agency that maintains standards for participating providers and determines whether each laboratory is in compliance with federal standards and any additional state regulations. [See 42 U.S.C. §1396a(9); 42 C.F.R. §431.610.] Each state agency develops its own procedures for approving providers that wish to be eligible to handle Medicaid patients. The general format of the procedure is that the provider must apply to the state agency for approval.

Q.7:9 How do state Medicaid programs typically reimburse clinical laboratory tests?

Each state administers its own Medicaid program and has considerable flexibility in doing so. Thus, it is impossible to generalize about Medicaid reimbursement requirements other than to review the federal requirements that all states must follow.

Medicaid is a "vendor payment" program. In other words, according to federal regulations, participation in the Medicaid program is limited to providers who accept as payment in full the amounts paid by the state Medicaid agency, plus any deductible, coinsurance, or other copayment required by the state Medicaid plan to be paid by the individual. Thus, all laboratories that provide services to Medicaid patients are paid directly by the Medicaid program. [42 C.F.R. §447.15]

Although the Medicaid regulations allow for limited patient cost-sharing through enrollment fees, premiums, deductibles, and coinsurance, these cost-sharing devices are subject to significant restrictions. For example, enrollment fees and premiums may not be charged to individuals who are defined as "categorically needy." Deductibles and copayment amounts may only be "nominal" and may not be imposed on certain categories of patients or certain categories of services. The Medicaid regulations also set certain upper limits for Medicaid cost-sharing amounts. These maximum amounts are established pursuant to a regulatory scale based on income and family size. [See 42 C.F.R. §§447.50-58.]

There is a provision of the Medicaid regulations that effectively places a floor (albeit a low one) below Medicaid reimbursement levels. This regulation establishes that the state Medicaid agency's payments must enlist enough providers so that medical services are available to Medicaid beneficiaries to the same extent as to the general population. [42 C.F.R. §447.204]

Finally, the Medicaid regulations provide that every state agency must furnish public notice of any significant proposed change in methods and standards for setting payment rates for services. [42 C.F.R. §447.205(a)]

Q.7:10 Does Medicaid reimburse as much as Medicare and private insurance for clinical laboratory tests?

Typically, the levels of Medicaid reimbursement for clinical laboratory tests and various other services fall below the levels established by Medicare and private insurance. As noted above, however, Medicaid payment amounts may not fall so low that they adversely affect the availability of services to Medicaid beneficiaries.

Q.7:11 What sanctions exist for violating Medicaid requirements?

In general, the sanctions for violating Medicaid requirements by receiving overpayments from the Medicaid program or engaging in activities that constitute fraud and abuse, and the specific activities subject to sanction, are the same as under the Medicare program. For a discussion of such activities and sanctions, see Chapter 2.

8

Blood Banks

Q.8:1 What types of blood-handling facilities are regulated?

There are four basic types of blood-handling facilities that are subject to regulation:

1. Blood banks,
2. Plasmapheresis centers,
3. Hospital transfusion services, and
4. Clinical laboratories.

Different regulatory requirements are triggered by the distinctions between these four types of facilities.

Q.8:2 What is a blood bank?

A *blood bank* is an establishment that stores a supply of human blood for future use by other individuals. Typically, a blood bank is involved in the collection, processing, testing, storage, and administration of human blood for use by others.

Q.8:3 What is a plasmapheresis center?

A *plasmapheresis center* is an establishment that performs plasmapheresis on paid donors, separating the donor's plasma (the fluid portion of human blood) from red blood cells and returning the red cells in a suspended solution immediately to the donor.

Q.8:4 What is a transfusion service?

A *transfusion service* is a facility located in a hospital that limits its blood handling to compatibility testing of processed blood with recipient's blood to ensure proper administration of blood to a patient.

Q.8:5 What is a clinical laboratory?

A *clinical laboratory* subject to the federal requirements for blood-handling facilities is one that routinely collects blood, performs required tests for processing blood, or performs required tests for plasmapheresis centers.

It should be noted that clinical laboratories that test blood or blood products in support of other registered blood establishments are excluded from the Food and Drug Administration (FDA) blood registration and inspection requirements if such facilities are inspected by the Health Care Financing Administration (HCFA) and approved for Medicare reimbursement. [21 C.F.R. §607.65]

Q.8:6 Who regulates blood-handling facilities?

Blood-handling facilities are regulated principally by the federal FDA, the independent federal agency that administers federal laws relating to such facilities.

Q.8:7 What are the major federal laws that regulate blood-handling facilities?

The major federal laws that regulate blood-handling facilities are the following. The federal Food, Drug, and Cosmetic Act (FDA Act) [21 U.S.C. §§331, 333, 360], requires registration and FDA inspection for blood banks and subjects such facilities to FDA regulatory requirements concerning manufacturing practices and product labeling. The Public Health Service Act (PHS Act), [42 U.S.C. §262], requires licensure and inspection of facilities that intend to exchange or sell blood or blood products interstate.

Q.8:8 What is the difference between licensure and registration of blood-handling facilities?

Licensure is a requirement of the PHS Act that applies to all establishments that propagate or manufacture biological products intended for sale, barter, or exchange either in the District of Columbia or interstate. [42 U.S.C. §262(a)] Failure to obtain a license prior to the manufacture of blood or blood products intended for trade interstate or in the District of Columbia is a violation of the PHS Act that is subject to punishment, including fines and imprisonment.

Registration is a requirement of the FDA Act applicable to "every person who owns or operates any establishment in any State engaged in the manufacture, preparation, propagation, compounding or processing of any drug or drugs . . . ." [21 U.S.C. §360] The federal courts have held that human blood or any blood component is considered a "drug" within the Act's definition of drugs. [*United States v. Calise*, 217 F. Supp. 705 (S.D.N.Y. 1962); *United States v. Steinschreiber*, 219 F. Supp. 373 (S.D.N.Y.), *aff'd*, 326 F.2d 759 (2d Cir. 1964)] Thus, all blood banks and other manufacturers of blood and blood products, even those operating intrastate, must register and file a product listing with the FDA.

In short, licensure and registration of blood-handling facilities are similar requirements applicable to similar facilities; however, licensure applies only to those facilities operating interstate or in the District of Columbia, whereas registration applies to all facilities, even those operating within a single state. The other major difference between the two requirements is the way in which they are administered and the related regulatory standards that apply to each.

Q.8:9 What facilities must hold an establishment license?

Under the PHS Act, 42 U.S.C. §262, and federal regulations implementing that law, 21 C.F.R. §601.10, every establishment that processes blood or blood products intended for interstate distribution must obtain both an establishment and a product license. To obtain an establishment license, a facility must have at least one licensable product available for inspection. The PHS Act requires that licenses may only be issued to those facilities that can demonstrate that both the establishment and its products meet standards designed to ensure the continued safety, purity, and potency of the products involved. [42 U.S.C. §262(d).]

Q.8:10 How are licensure requirements administered and enforced?

Blood establishment and product licensure requirements are administered and enforced by the FDA, which has promulgated detailed regulations establishing the standards that facilities and products must meet in order to be eligible for licenses. These standards include minimum good manufacturing practices (GMPs) for blood and blood components [21 C.F.R. §§606.3-606.170]; general standards for biological products [21 C.F.R. §§610.1-610.65]; standards concerning hepatitis testing [21 C.F.R. §610.50]; standards concerning expiration dates [1 C.F.R. §610.53]; labeling standards [21 C.F.R. §§610.60-610.65]; and requirements for personnel, physical plant, and records [21 C.F.R. §§600.10–600.12.]

Typically, the FDA issues a single establishment license to cover all locations of an entity that meets these standards. Once a license is issued by the FDA, it need not be renewed, since it continues in effect until suspended or revoked by the FDA. However, licensed establishments must report all important changes, including those involving location, equipment, management, and responsible personnel, and receive approval from the FDA for such changes 30 days in advance. Procedures for suspension or revocation of an establishment license for violation of the required standard are set forth at 21 C.F.R. §§601.5–601.9.

To receive a product license, the applicant must submit data demonstrating that the manufactured product meets prescribed standards of safety, purity, and potency. [21 C.F.R. §601.2] The product licensure process consists of a submission of acceptable data; a full description of the establishment's manufacturing methods; representative samples of the product; and specimens of the labels, enclosures, and containers proposed to be used for the product. If the product is a new one, or produced by means of a new method of manufacturing, the data required to be submitted by the FDA prior to product licensure are much more substantial and complex. [See 21 C.F.R. §§601 *et seq*.]

All establishments that seek establishment licensure are subject to FDA inspection [21 C.F.R. §600.20]. Licensed establishments must be inspected at least once every two years, with or without notice. [21 C.F.R. §600.21] Generally, the FDA conducts these inspections without advance notice. Inspection requirements apply to both establishment licensure and product licensure.

Q.8:11 What facilities are subject to registration requirements?

All blood establishments are required by the FDA to register and file a product listing with FDA annually. [21 U.S.C. §360] The registration requirements, as noted above, apply to wholly intrastate, as well as to interstate, distributors of blood and blood products. However, as a condition of licensure under the PHS Act, a blood establishment that intends to distribute blood or blood products interstate must register under the FDA Act.

It should be noted that the term *establishment* is defined more narrowly for registration purposes than for licensure purposes. For registration purposes, an establishment is defined at 21 C.F.R. §607.3(c) as "a place of business under one management at one general physical location." In other words, several separate physical locations may be termed *establishments* and required to *register* individually, even though all of these locations together may obtain a common, single establishment *license*.

Q.8:12 How are registration requirements administered and enforced?

Technically, all facilities that manufacture or engage in any significant step in the manufacture or distribution of blood or blood products must register. Thus, all blood banks and plasmapheresis centers are required to register annually and be inspected by the FDA. However, the responsibility for inspecting Medicare-approved laboratories and transfusion services has been transferred from the FDA to HCFA. [21 C.F.R. §607.65(f), (g)] Consequently, hospital transfusion services that do not routinely draw and process blood, and clinical laboratories that test blood products in support of other registered establishments, are no longer registered or inspected by the FDA, provided that they have been approved by HCFA for Medicare reimbursement. [21 C.F.R. §607.65]

Thus, HCFA is the sole inspector of certain Medicare-approved transfusion services and independent laboratories. However, in assuming this inspection role, HCFA adopted by cross-reference FDA regulations relating to syphilis serology testing, blood grouping, antibody detection and identification, and compatibility testing; collection, processing, and distribution; dating; and hepatitis testing. [See 21 C.F.R. §§610.53, 610.40, Part 606, and Part 640.] As a result, affected transfusion services and clinical laboratories, while no longer separately inspected by the FDA, must still meet applicable FDA requirements.

Annual registration is required for covered facilities between November 15 and December 31 of each year. [21 C.F.R. §607.21] The initial registration must include a list of all blood products to be distributed. After the first registration, that products list must be updated every June and December. Product listing information may be submitted by a parent company for all registered establishments that it owns and operates. Registered establishments are inspected every other year. When the inspection is performed by the FDA, the agency typically uses the same procedures, forms, and requirements as used when inspecting licensed blood establishments.

Q.8:13 What requirements apply to the labeling of blood and blood products?

All facilities that collect, process, distribute, or administer blood or blood products must comply with FDA labeling requirements.

Certain labeling information must appear on all whole blood and products derived from whole blood. That labeling information includes the following:

- The name of the product;
- The name, address, registration number, and (if applicable) license number of the manufacturer;
- The donor pool or lot number relating the unit to the donor;
- The expiration date;
- A statement classifying the donor as paid or volunteer;
- Product volume information;
- Recommended storage temperature;
- The ABO and Rh groups of the donor;
- Information concerning results of hepatitis B testing;
- The volume of anticoagulant;
- The name of the applicable anticoagulant; and
- Specific statements prescribed in FDA regulations.

[See 21 C.F.R. §§606.120–606.121.] Additional specific labeling requirements apply to each separate blood product.

Q.8:14 What are the labeling requirements for emergency blood shipments?

When a blood bank or hospital transfusion service distributes or administers blood and blood products in emergencies, without completing the required tests, the label must include the statement: "FOR EMERGENCY USE ONLY BY ________"; the results of any blood group, Rh factor, syphilis, hepatitis surface B antigen test, or human immunodeficiency virus (HIV) antibody test completed prior to shipment; and the identification of any of these required tests that were not completed prior to shipment. [21 C.F.R. §606.121(h)]

Q.8:15 What requirements apply to the dating of blood shipments?

FDA regulations that apply to the labeling of blood and blood products include specific requirements for labeling information concerning expiration dates. The label of any blood or blood product must bear the product's expiration date. The expiration date is determined by identifying the date of manufacture and then adding to that the product's dating period.

The date of manufacture is the date of initiation of the last valid potency test, where potency tests are required. [21 C.F.R. §610.50(a)] For products not subject to official potency tests, the date of manufacture is the date of extraction, the date of solution, the date of cessation of growth, or the date of final sterile filtration of a bulk solution, whichever is applicable. [21 C.F.R. §610.50(b)]

For blood, the date of manufacture is the date when the blood was collected. For blood components, the date of manufacture is the date of collection of the blood from which the component was prepared.

The product's dating period is the "reasonable period beyond which the product cannot be expected beyond reasonable doubt to yield its specific results and retain its safety, purity and potency, provided the product is maintained at the recommended temperatures." [21 C.F.R. §610.53(a)] The expiration date is the date on which the dating period ends. [21 C.F.R. §600.3(m)] Specific dating periods for individual products are set forth in the regulations. [See 21 C.F.R. §610.53.]

Q.8:16 What requirements apply to the manufacturing processes of blood-handling facilities?

All facilities, whether licensed or registered, that handle blood and blood components must conform to the applicable GMPs in FDA regulations at 21 C.F.R. §§606.3–606.170. These GMPs cover the following aspects of facility performance:

- Personnel,
- Physical plant,
- Equipment,
- Supplies and reagents,
- Standard operating procedures manual,

- Labeling,
- Laboratory controls,
- Compatibility testing, and
- Records.

Q.8:17 How do manufacturing requirements differ depending on the specific blood product involved?

In addition to the general GMPs that apply to all blood and blood products, specific standards apply to the manufacture or processing of certain individual products. These individual products, including their definitions and the regulatory sections setting forth standards that apply to them, are as follows.

Whole blood is blood collected from human donors for transfusion to human recipients. [21 C.F.R. §640.1] The standards applicable to the collection and processing of whole blood are found at 21 C.F.R. §§640.1–640.6.

Red blood cells are those red blood cells remaining after separating plasma from human blood. [21 C.F.R. §640.10.] The specific requirements for production of red blood cells are found at 21 C.F.R. §§640.10–640.17.

Platelets consist of platelets collected from one unit of blood and resuspended in an appropriate volume of original plasma. [21 C.F.R. §640.20(a)] The standards for the production of platelets are set forth at 21 C.F.R. §§640.20-640.27.

Plasma is the fluid portion of one unit of human blood intended for intravenous use that, in a closed system, has been collected, stabilized against clotting, and separated from the red blood cells. [21 C.F.R. §640.30(a)] The standards that apply to the production of plasma are set forth at 21 C.F.R. §§640.30–640.34.

Cryoprecipitated antihemophilic factor (AHF) is a preparation of AHF factor obtained from a single unit of plasma collected and processed in a closed system. [21 C.F.R. §640.50(a)] The requirements that apply to the preparation of cryoprecipitated AHF are set forth at 21 C.F.R. §§640.50–640.56.

Q.8:18 What requirements apply to the donors of blood products?

FDA regulations contain a number of requirements that must be met by facilities that produce blood products drawn from donors. Facilities that collect whole blood must establish that each donor is suitable each time blood is collected from that person. Suitability should be determined by a physician or by supervised personnel trained to determine suitability. In order to be considered suitable as a blood donor, a person may not serve as a source of whole blood more than once in eight weeks, unless a physician specifically requires otherwise. Donors also must be in good health and meet certain standards concerning medical history and clinical indications set forth in the regulations. For more detail on donor suitability requirements, see 21 C.F.R. §640.3.

The regulations also contain specific standards applicable to donors of blood to be used in the preparation of specific blood products.

Q.8:19 What requirements are there for the process of collecting blood from donors?

All blood banks and facilities that collect whole blood must also comply with specific regulatory requirements concerning collection procedures. These requirements relate to the nature of containers, container identification, preparation of the donor's skin, sterile blood collection methodology, the collection of pilot samples for laboratory testing, and formulas for anticoagulant solutions. For more detail on these blood collection requirements, see 21 C.F.R. §640.4.

The FDA regulations further require that, immediately after collection, blood must be placed in storage at certain recommended temperatures, which generally range from 1°C to 6°C. [See 21 C.F.R. §640.4(i).]

Q.8:20 What tests must be performed on blood drawn from donors?

Facilities that collect blood must perform certain required tests in their own laboratories or through independent clinical laboratories on contract. The blood must meet the following requirements:

- Be tested for syphilis and yield negative;
- Be tested for determination of blood grouping by at least two methods or lots that agree;
- Be tested to determine Rh factors and receive certain labeling based on the results;
- Be tested for sterility;
- Be inspected for abnormal color or physical appearance and reveal no abnormality or suspicion of microbial contamination; and
- Be tested for hepatitis B surface antigen and antibody to HIV.

[See 21 C.F.R. §§640.5, 610.40, 610.41, 610.45.]

Q.8:21 Are there specific standards for the testing of blood and blood products for hepatitis?

As noted above, each donation of blood or blood products must be tested for the presence of hepatitis B surface antigen. Federal regulations establish requirements for such testing, including the following:

- The testing methodology;
- The antibodies to be used in testing;
- Testing procedures that conform to manufacturers' package inserts;
- Restrictions on use of blood or blood products that test reactive;
- Exclusion from donors of persons testing positive, or known to have previously tested positive, for hepatitis B surface antigen; and
- Labeling on emergency shipments of blood products before completion of required hepatitis B surface antigen tests.

[See 21 C.F.R. §§610.40, 610.41.]

Q.8:22 Are there specific standards for the testing of blood and blood products for HIV?

As noted previously, each donation of human blood or blood components intended for use in preparing a blood product must be tested for antibody to HIV. The FDA regulations establish standards for HIV testing that relate to the testing product; the emergency issuance of products before the completion of testing; and restrictions on use of blood or blood components that tested "repeatedly reactive" to HIV antibody or that were collected from a donor whose blood is known to be repeatedly reactive. [See 21 C.F.R. §610.45.]

Q.8:23 What are the most important occupational safety requirements that apply to blood-handling facilities, and by what agency are these requirements enforced?

Perhaps the most important occupational safety requirements that apply to blood-handling facilities are those contained in the "bloodborne pathogens" regulations issued and enforced by the Occupational Safety and Health Administration (OSHA). These regulations are discussed in greater detail in Chapter 11, **Q.11:46** and **Q.11:47**. Generally, they prescribe actions that employers must undertake to protect workers from actual or potential exposure to HIV, hepatitis B, and other infectious materials.

The regulations include requirements for operating procedures, personal protective equipment, protective clothing, and hepatitis B vaccinations. They incorporate the Centers for Disease Control and Prevention's (CDC's) "universal precautions" for the protection of health care workers who have had exposure to HIV. [See *Morbidity and Mortality Weekly Report* (June 24, 1988).]

Q.8:24 Can a blood-handling facility be liable for harm to a patient who has contracted hepatitis or acquired immunodeficiency syndrome (AIDS) as a result of a blood transfusion?

Patients who have contracted hepatitis or AIDS through blood transfusions have often sued the hospital or blood bank that provided the blood used in the transfusion. Typically, such cases have proceeded under three theories of liability: (1) strict liability for a defective product; (2) breach of warranty that a product is free of defects; and (3) negligence in collecting or screening of blood or informing patients of transfusion-related risks.

The first two theories, strict liability and breach of warranty, have largely been eliminated as grounds for lawsuits by statute in virtually all states. These statutes, known as "blood shield" laws, treat the transfer of blood as a "service" rather than the sale of a "product," and make the theories of strict liability and breach of warranty inapplicable because they are based on defective "product" rather than "service" concepts.

Thus, the negligence theory is the only one that remains valid as the basis for a lawsuit against a laboratory or hospital for transfusion-related injuries. Under the negligence theory, a plaintiff claims that the blood establishment did not meet the required standard of care in the screening or testing of blood donors or the blood collected, or did not provide the transfusion recipient sufficient information concerning possible transmission of diseases to allow the patient to give informed consent to the transfusion. Consequently, the ability of plaintiffs to win such lawsuits has been closely related to the state of medical technology and knowledge at the time the blood was collected and transfused.

Q.8:25 What is an example of a case involving hospital or blood bank liability for transfused blood?

One illustrative case is *Hoemke v. New York Blood Center*, 912 F.2d 550 (2d Cir. 1990). In that case, the federal appellate court held that a hospital blood bank whose blood caused a patient to contract AIDS after a 1981 transfusion during surgery did not breach any duty of care owed to the patient by failing to institute procedures for autologous or directed blood transfusions, and the blood center did not breach a standard of reasonable care by failing to screen out gay male donors or failing to administer certain laboratory tests on its blood supply. The court noted that at the time of the transfusion in 1981, AIDS had not yet been discovered to be a bloodborne disease, and there was no evidence suggesting that the unordered laboratory tests might identify the AIDS virus in blood.

9

AIDS and the Laboratory

Q.9:1 How is AIDS defined medically?

AIDS (acquired immune deficiency syndrome) is a disease characterized by progressive weakening of the immune system and ultimate fatality. As of January 1993, the clinical definition of AIDS established by the U.S. Centers for Disease Control and Prevention (CDC) was a positive response to a test for the human immunodeficiency virus (HIV) plus one or more of the following conditions:

- The fungal infectious disease coccidioidomycosis,
- HIV encephalopathy,
- Histoplasmosis,
- The bowel disorder isosporiasis,
- Kaposi's sarcoma,
- Lymphoma of the brain,
- Non-Hodgkin's lymphoma,
- Mycobacterial disease,
- Mycobacterial tuberculosis outside the lungs,
- Recurrent salmonella,
- HIV wasting syndrome,
- Pulmonary tuberculosis,
- Recurrent pneumonia,
- Invasive cervical cancer, or
- A T4 (CD 4) cell count below 200.

Q.9:2 What causes AIDS?

AIDS is caused by a virus now known as human immunodeficiency virus type I (HIV-I), known commonly as HIV. HIV is a member of a group of viruses known as human retroviruses. Its genetic material is ribonucleic acid (RNA) rather than deoxyribonucleic acid (DNA), the genetic material found in most living organisms. The virus particle is composed of a core containing the RNA and viral enzymes surrounded by an envelope consisting of lipids and proteins.

Because they lack the cellular machinery necessary to reproduce, all viruses must reproduce intracellularly, that is, within the host cell. HIV replicates in human macrophages and T4 lymphocytes, two types of human cells that are vital components of the immune system. T4 lymphocytes and a few other cell types have protein molecules on their surfaces called CD4 antigens or receptors. HIV particles bind with the CD4 receptor sites of the hosts' cells and then release their viral RNA. The RNA is then transcribed by viral enzymes into double-stranded DNA that is incorporated into the DNA of the host cell. The viral DNA then serves as a template to produce more virus particles.

A transcription of RNA to DNA is the reverse of what occurs in most organisms, and it is for this reason that HIV is called a *retrovirus*. The process occurs with the aid of the viral enzyme reverse transcriptase, which is considered to be a marker for retrovirus production. HIV gradually depletes the number of cells that are essential for host immune function, making the infected individual increasingly susceptible to opportunistic infections.

Circulating macrophages are also considered a reservoir as well as another target for HIV infection. Since macrophages can circulate freely throughout the body, they may actually transport HIV to the brain, leading to neurologic complications.

Q.9:3 When and how was AIDS discovered in the United States?

In June of 1981, the first cases of a previously unknown disease were reported in the United States. Investigators described an unusual illness characterized by pneumocystis carinii pneumonia (PCP) and Kaposi's sarcoma (KS) that developed in young, homosexual men without a known underlying disease or cause for immunosuppression.

By early 1982, 159 cases of the new disease, now known as AIDS, had been identified in 15 states, the District of Columbia, and two foreign countries. All but one of the victims were men, and over 92% of them were homosexual or bisexual men. By the end of 1982, cases of AIDS were reported among children, intravenous drug users, blood transfusion recipients, hemophilia patients treated with clotting factor concentrates, and Haitians. In 1983, the disease was also documented among female sexual partners of male intravenous drug users in the United States and among Africans. By the end of 1985, all 50 states, the District of Columbia, and 3 U.S. territories had reported AIDS cases.

Q.9:4 When was HIV identified as the cause of AIDS?

During 1983 and 1984, French and American scientists independently isolated a human virus associated with AIDS. Dr. Luc Montagnier and his coworkers at the Institute Pasteur in Paris called the virus *lymphadenopathy associated virus* (LAV). Dr. Robert Gallo and his coworkers at the National Cancer Institute identified the virus as human T-cell lymphotropic virus type III, eventually isolated by these researchers as the causative agent for AIDS.

Q.9:5 What are the clinical manifestations of AIDS?

HIV adversely affects the immune system, rendering the infected individual vulnerable to a wide range of clinical disorders. These conditions, some of which tend to recur, can be aggressive, rapidly progressive, difficult to treat, and less responsive to traditional modes of treatment than disorders affecting HIV-negative persons. They include the disorders identified in the CDC's definition of AIDS. (See **Q.9:1**, above.) These disorders eventually lead to the death of the HIV-infected patient.

Q.9:6 What is the progression of AIDS?

The CDC has divided the progression of AIDS into several stages, according to types of infections or symptoms reported. These stages are Groups I through IV.

- **Group I:** Within a month after exposure, an individual may experience acute retroviral syndrome, the first clinical evidence of HIV infection. This is a mononucleosis-like condition with signs and symptoms that can include fever, lymphadenopathy, myalgia, arthralgia, diarrhea, fatigue, and rash. Acute retroviral syndrome is usually self-limiting and is followed or accompanied by the development of antibodies to HIV.
- **Group II:** Although most persons infected with HIV develop antibodies to the virus within 6 to 12 weeks after exposure, most of these individuals are asymptomatic for months to years following infection. However, these persons are capable of transmitting the virus to others throughout this time.
- **Group III:** Although no other signs or symptoms are experienced, some HIV-infected patients will develop a persistent, generalized lymphadenopathy that lasts more than 3 months.
- **Group IV:** Epidemiologic data indicate that most persons who are infected with HIV will eventually develop AIDS. AIDS can result in severe opportunistic infections that an individual with a normal immune system would only rarely experience, as well as a wide range of neurologic and oncogenic or neoplastic processes. The clinical manifestations of patients in this group may vary extensively. Some of these patients may experience "constitutional disease," also known as "HIV wasting syndrome," which may be characterized by severe, involuntary weight loss, chronic diarrhea, constant or intermittent weakness, and fever for 30 days or longer. This syndrome in and of itself may result in death.

Individuals with AIDS may also develop HIV encephalopathy, dementia, myelopathy, or peripheral neuropathy. This may occur when HIV infects mononuclear cells present in the cerebrospinal fluids surrounding the brain and spinal cord or infects these cells within the brain or spinal cord. Persons with dementia experience varying degrees of cognitive disability or impairment of intellectual function and motor disability or dysfunction. Effects ranging from apathy and depression to memory loss and severe dementia may interfere with a person's occupation, as well as activities of daily living, and can ultimately be fatal. In addition, the virus is capable of affecting the peripheral nervous system, causing severe pain and weakness or numbness in the limbs (peripheral neuropathy).

Q.9:7 What are the prevalences of AIDS and HIV infection in the U.S. population today?

According to the CDC, 315,390 cases of AIDS were reported in the United States between June 1981 and June 1993. The 1993 figure represents an increase of over 200% from the total reported in the previous year.

The CDC's estimate of the number of HIV-positive persons in the United States is 1,000,000 persons, or 1 in 250 Americans, as of October 1, 1993. A 1993 estimate by the National Center for Health Statistics is that 300,000 to 1 million Americans are infected.

Q.9:8 What is the evidence of occupational transmission of HIV?

Occupational transmission of HIV has been documented in health care workers. As of May 1990, there were at least 65 case reports of health care workers whose HIV infections are associated with occupational exposure. Among these are 30 case reports that have been individually published in the scientific literature. Eighteen of these cases seroconverted following a documented exposure incident. Thirteen of the seroconversions were caused by parenteral exposure to blood or blood-containing body fluids (11 by needlesticks and 2 by cuts with a sharp object). Five seroconversions involved blood contamination of mucous membranes or nonintact skin, and one was due to parenteral exposure to concentrated HIV virus. The dates of seroconversion could not be documented for the remaining 12 individually published cases because no baseline serologic data had been obtained.

The published cases of HIV infection associated with occupational exposure represent a spectrum of health care personnel including, among others, nurses, laboratory workers, and a dentist. Of 25 recently published cases, HIV status was determined by HIV-antibody testing. Baseline blood samples analyzed for HIV-antibody revealed that at least 18 of the individuals were not infected with HIV at the time of the exposure incident. Subsequent blood tests determined that eventually all of the 18 seroconverted to an HIV-positive antibody status, indicating the presence of HIV infection. All 25 denied other known risk factors for HIV infection, but in cases where the baseline serologic data were unknown, other modes of transmission cannot be ruled out entirely. However, all cases were investigated for risk factors, and none were identified.

Q.9:9 What are some examples of HIV infection associated with occupational exposure in a clinical laboratory worker?

Two examples of clinical laboratory workers who had occupational exposure to HIV are as follows.

A female phlebotomist reported that blood spattered on her face and in her mouth when the top of a 10-mL vacuum blood collection tube flew off while she was collecting a patient's blood, which subsequently tested HIV-positive. The phlebotomist was wearing gloves and glasses, and reported that no blood got in her eyes. She reported no open wounds, but did have facial acne. She washed off the blood immediately after exposure. Her blood tested HIV-negative one day after exposure and eight weeks after exposure. However, when donating blood nine months after exposure, she was HIV-antibody positive. She denied having other known risk factors for HIV.

A female medical technologist was exposed to a blood spill that covered most of her hands and forearms while she was manipulating an apheresis machine, a machine that separates blood components, retains some, and returns the remainder to the donor.

Although the medical technologist was not wearing gloves, she did not report any open wounds on her hands or any mucous membrane exposure. However, she did have dermatitis on her ear and may have touched that ear. Eight weeks after the incident, she experienced symptoms of acute retroviral syndrome (see above). She was HIV-negative five days after exposure, but three months after exposure, she was HIV-antibody positive. She denied having other known risk factors for AIDS. Her husband also denied any risk factors for AIDS and tested HIV-seronegative.

Q.9:10 How is AIDS transmitted?

HIV has been isolated from human blood, semen, breast milk, vaginal secretions, saliva, tears, urine, cerebrospinal fluid, and amniotic fluid; however, epidemiologic evidence implicates only blood, semen, vaginal secretions, and breast milk in the transmission of the virus. Documented modes of HIV transmission include the following:

- Engaging in sexual intercourse with an HIV-infected person;
- Using needles contaminated with the virus;
- Having parenteral, mucous membrane, or nonintact skin contact with HIV-infected blood, blood components, or blood products;
- Receiving transplants of HIV-infected organs and tissues including bone, or transfusions of HIV-infected blood;
- Receiving it through semen used for artificial insemination and perinatal transmission (from mother to child around the time of birth).

HIV is not transmitted by casual contact. Studies evaluating nearly 500 household contacts of individuals diagnosed with AIDS reveal no cases of HIV infection of household members who had no other risk factors for the virus (including no sexual contact with or exposure to blood from the infected person).

For example, one recent study examined household members who had lived with a person with AIDS for at least 3 months and within an 18-month period prior to the onset of symptoms in the infected person (during which time infection was presumably present). Other household members had been unaware of the infected individual's HIV status and had not taken precautions during this time. The study produced no evidence that HIV was transmitted by shaking hands or talking; by sharing food, eating utensils, plates, drinking glasses, or towels; by sharing the same house or household facilities; or by "personal interactions expected of family members" including hugging and kissing on the cheek or lips.

Other studies have shown that HIV is not transmitted by mosquitoes or other animals.

Q.9:11 What are the risks of HIV transmission in different types of exposures?

The risk of infection following receipt of transfused blood from an HIV-infected donor is approximately 90%. The risk of perinatal transmission from an HIV-infected mother is estimated at 30 to 50% or higher.

Q.9:12 Other than the method of exposure, what factors may affect the likelihood of HIV transmission?

In addition to the type of exposure, other variables contributing to the likelihood of HIV transmission may include the susceptibility of the host; the virulence of the particular virus strain; the stage of infection of the source; and the size of inoculum, or the actual amount of the virus, that the individual contacts.

Q.9:13 Have there been any studies of the specific risk of HIV occurrence in laboratory workers?

Yes. Weiss and coworkers conducted a prospective study to assess the risk of HIV in laboratory workers. [See Preamble to

Occupational Safety and Health Administration (OSHA) bloodborne pathogens regulations, 56 Fed. Reg. 64020 (December 6, 1991).] In this study, invitations to participate were issued to workers with possible exposure risk in 15 laboratory facilities from 6 states. Of the 265 subjects studied, 225 had laboratory exposure (including 99 who worked with concentrated HIV and 126 who worked with blood containing HIV, noninfectious viral proteins, or cloned viral DNA), 30 worked with AIDS patients in support of the laboratory, and 10 were clerical staff working in the laboratory environment.

Of the 225 laboratory workers, 10 reported 1 or more episodes of parenteral exposure to HIV, including needlesticks or cuts, and 35 reported 1 or more episodes of skin contact with HIV. Participants completed a questionnaire focusing on workplace exposure to human retroviruses, biosafety precautions used at the facility and by the subject, accidents occurring in the laboratory or other areas, and nonoccupational factors such as drug use, sexual activity, and transfusion history. Eight (3%) of the 265 reported nonoccupational risk factors for the virus. Of the 225 workers with laboratory exposure, 10 reported parenteral virus exposure, and 35 reported 1 or more skin contacts. Thirteen workers reported that they did not wear gloves at all times when working with HIV-infected material.

Blood samples from all subjects were analyzed for HIV antibodies by enzyme-linked immunosorbant assay and confirmed by tests such as immunoblots and radioimmune assays (see below). One individual who worked with concentrated HIV-I was seropositive for the virus upon entering the study. The HIV isolated from the subject's blood was shown to be genetically identical to a strain of HIV used in the laboratory, thus strongly implicating occupational exposure as the source of infection. The authors of the study concluded that the most plausible source of exposure was contact of the worker's gloved hand with culture supernatant fluid containing concentrated virus, followed by inapparent exposure to skin. No HIV seroconversions were identified in the study participants during the period of prospective follow-up.

The authors of the study calculated on the basis of their research that the rate of HIV infection was 0.48 per 100 person-years for laboratory personnel in the study.

Q.9:14 How is HIV identified in serologic testing?

Infection with HIV is generally identified through testing the blood for the presence of HIV antibodies. HIV antibody tests were first licensed for use in the United States in 1985 and have been used routinely to screen donated blood, blood components, and blood products, and by physicians and clinics to diagnose HIV infection in patients. The military also uses the antibody test to screen recruit applicants and active duty personnel for HIV infection.

Although the antibodies do not appear to defend or protect the host against HIV, they serve as markers of viral infection. Most people infected with HIV have detectable antibodies with 6 months of infection, with the majority generating detectable antibodies between 6 and 12 weeks after exposure.

Q.9:15 What specific tests are used to identify HIV?

The enzyme-linked immunosorbant assay (ELISA or EIA) technique used to detect HIV antibodies is sensitive, economical, and easy to perform. However, as with all laboratory determinations, this test can produce a false-positive result (i.e., give a positive result when HIV antibody is not present). Therefore, current public health recommendations include repeating this assay if the first result is positive and, if the second result is also positive, validating the assay with a different test, usually employing the Western blot technique. A positive EIA test and a positive Western blot result indicate the presence of HIV antibodies and HIV infection.

One recently developed HIV testing method uses the polymerase chain reaction (PCR) technique. This test detects integrated viral DNA rather than antibody, and it may have the potential to detect HIV infection earlier than do antibody tests.

Q.9:16 Is it possible to do home testing for HIV?

Currently, the federal Food and Drug Administration (FDA) has not approved any method for home testing for the HIV virus.

Because clinical laboratory tests that have not been approved by the FDA cannot be marketed in the United States, it is illegal for home HIV tests to be sold in the United States, and therefore not feasible for home HIV testing to be conducted at the present time.

Q.9:17 Is clinical laboratory testing for AIDS or HIV regulated?

Yes. Although the federal government does not regulate HIV testing specifically, an increasing number of states have enacted statutes that regulate in some way testing for the HIV virus. Among the states that have enacted such laws are New York, California, Florida, Illinois, Maine, Massachusetts, New Jersey, North Carolina, and Ohio.

Q.9:18 What aspects of HIV testing are regulated by the states?

State laws affecting HIV testing vary in breadth and specificity. Generally, they cover the following:

- Test requests;
- Pretest counseling;
- Qualifications required of the testing laboratory;
- The products used in testing;
- Confirmatory testing;
- The reporting of test results;
- Posttest counseling;
- Record keeping; and
- Public health reporting.

Q.9:19 What requirements do states typically impose on clinical laboratories testing for HIV?

As noted above, state laws vary in the degree to which they regulate HIV testing. For example, Texas merely requires that HIV testing programs offered in Texas register with the state and meet certain limited requirements for post-test counseling of testing subjects, itemize charges for testing and counseling on bills, and report aggregate HIV test results to local authorities.

The New York law, on the other hand, is extremely comprehensive. It requires, among other things, that

- An HIV test be ordered by a physician or other person authorized by law to order tests;
- Written informed consent to the testing be obtained from the test subject;
- Pretest counseling be provided;
- Testing laboratories hold a state permit to perform testing;
- Confirmatory testing be performed;
- Laboratories permitted to perform confirmatory testing (as opposed to screening tests) be entities in the public sector;
- Testing employ kits approved by the FDA and acceptable to the New York Department of Health;
- Disclosure of test results be limited, generally to the physician ordering the test and the test subject with his or her written consent;
- The person ordering the test provide post-test counseling on specific topics;
- Billing for HIV tests use authorized codes and conceal the identity of the test as an HIV test;
- Aggregate test results be kept on file and reported to the department of health; and
- The testing laboratory or other entity running the testing program maintain specific procedures to guarantee the confidentiality of HIV-related information.

Q.9:20 What requirements do states typically impose regarding the disclosure of HIV test results?

Again, the state laws vary in the nature and degree of regulation they impose on HIV testing. As to disclosure of HIV test results, however, most state laws reflect a common policy that recognizes that disclosure of HIV-related information may result in discrimination and other injury to the test subject; therefore, the disclosure of test results should be strictly limited. Some states require that HIV testing be anonymous. Additionally, many states that regulate HIV testing impose strict limitations on the disclosure of HIV test results.

New Jersey's law is a good example. This statute, N.J.S. §26.5C-8, provides that, absent the test subject's prior written informed consent, disclosure of HIV testing results may be made only under the following circumstances:

- To qualified personnel for purposes of conducting scientific research under certain limited conditions;
- To qualified personnel for purposes of conducting management or financial audits or program evaluation, provided the release of identifying information to such personnel is vital to the audit or evaluation;
- To qualified personnel involved in medical education or the diagnosis and treatment of the test subject;
- To the department of health as required by state or federal law;
- Pursuant to rules and regulations adopted by the state commissioner of health for purposes of disease prevention and control; and
- In other instances authorized by state or federal law.

Q.9:21 How do state regulatory schemes deal with reporting of AIDS and HIV infection?

States increasingly view AIDS as a public health crisis and responsibility. Consequently, well over half of the states in the United States require some form of reporting of HIV test results or AIDS cases. Roughly half of these states require specific reporting by name in order to facilitate the notification and counseling of partners of HIV-infected persons in order to help stem the spread of the disease. The other half require only anonymous, aggregate reporting of total numbers of positive HIV tests in order to avoid disclosure of individuals' HIV-positive status and prevent any potential discrimination or other harm likely to result from disclosure of such status.

Q.9:22 What are the workplace safety requirements related to HIV?

The principal workplace safety requirements related to HIV are those contained in the OSHA's "bloodborne pathogens" regulations, which are intended to eliminate or minimize occupational exposure to hepatitis B virus (HBV) and HIV and other bloodborne pathogens. These regulations are also discussed in Chapter 11. Generally, they require that employers do the following:

- Adopt the Centers for Disease Control and Prevention's (CDC's) "universal precautions," which include specific steps that should be taken regarding work processes and practices to minimize exposure to bloodborne pathogens;
- Implement certain specified engineering and work practice controls;
- Require and facilitate the use of personal protective equipment by workers;
- Follow certain waste disposal practices; and
- Generally develop and implement a written Exposure Control Plan to minimize risk of occupational exposure to blood and infectious materials.

[See 56 Fed. Reg. 64004 *et seq.* (December 6, 1991), 29 C.F.R. §1910.1030 *et seq.*]

Q.9:23 Can a health care provider refuse to treat or provide services to a person who is HIV-positive?

Such refusal of treatment is probably both illegal and medically unethical.

In addition to provisions of some state laws that may forbid health care providers to refuse treatment to HIV-positive persons, such refusal of treatment would likely be prohibited under the federal Americans with Disabilities Act (ADA), 42 U.S.C. §12101 *et seq*. Title III of the ADA requires that "public accommodations" be made physically accessible to persons with disabilities and prohibits eligibility criteria for goods and services that tend to screen out individuals with disabilities from fully enjoying any of the benefits of such services. Providers of medical services are defined to be among the "public accommodations" covered by Title III. Eligibility criteria for "public accommodations" are acceptable under the ADA only when they are necessary for the provision of the goods and services being offered. Thus, for any provider of medical services to impose a limitation or condition that denied treatment to HIV-positive persons would probably be treated as a violation of the ADA.

Additionally, medical ethics opinions developed by the American Medical Association (AMA) deem it unethical for a physician to refuse treatment to an HIV-positive person. Thus, a 1992 Opinion of the AMA's Council on Ethical and Judicial Affairs states the following:

> *HIV INFECTED PATIENTS AND PHYSICIANS*. A physician may not ethically refuse to treat a patient whose condition is within the physician's current realm of competence solely because the patient is seropositive for HIV. Persons who are seropositive should not be subjected to discrimination based on fear or prejudice.
>
> When physicians are unable to provide the services required by an HIV-infected patient, they should make appropriate referrals to those physicians or facilities equipped to provide such services. [American Medical Association, Council on Ethical and Judicial Affairs, *Code of Medical Ethics Current Opinions*, Opinion No. 9.131 (1992)]

Q.9:24 What laws apply when a clinical laboratory employee tests positive for HIV?

When a clinical laboratory employee tests positive for HIV, the major laws that come into play are state laws restricting disclosure of HIV-related information (see above); the federal ADA, which prohibits discrimination in employment against persons with disabilities, specifically including HIV-positive persons; and the laws of some states, such as California, which are similar to the federal ADA. For employers who are public-sector entities or who receive benefits under federal programs, such as Medicare or Medicaid benefits, the Rehabilitation Act of 1973, which imposes the same requirements as the ADA, also comes into play.

The state laws that limit disclosure of HIV-related information are generally quite specific but vary from state to state and should be consulted directly to make sure the specific provisions are observed. Generally, these laws impose severe limits on disclosure of HIV-related information, including test results, to persons other than the test subject and his or her physician without the test subject's consent.

The ADA prohibits employers from discriminating in hiring, firing, transferring, or work conditions against employees with disabilities and also requires employers to provide "reasonable accommodations" to permit such employees to continue performing their desired jobs notwithstanding their disabilities. Regulations promulgated under the ADA also prohibit discrimination against persons with disabilities with respect to employment fringe benefits. [29 C.F.R. §1630.4(f)]

In addition, a guidance document issued by the Equal Employment Opportunity Commission (EEOC), which enforces ADA requirements, makes clear that an employer can be liable for discrimination in health insurance from an insurance company, health maintenance organization, or other third-party insurer or administrator. The guidance document says that insurance plan distinctions directly based on disabilities generally violate the ADA; employment decisions affecting persons with disabilities may not be motivated by concerns about the impact of an individual's disability on the employer's health insurance plan; employees with disabilities must be afforded the same access to health insurance as persons without disabilities; and employers may not make employment decisions based on the likely health insurance impact of persons with whom that employee has a relationship. See EEOC, *Interim Enforcement Guidance,* on the application of the ADA to disability-based distinctions in employer-provided health insurance (June 9, 1993).

Q.9:25 What limitations can a laboratory employer safely place on an HIV-positive employee?

The mere fact that an employee has tested for HIV will probably not permit the employer to make any changes in the conditions of that person's employment, such as firing, job transfer, and so forth. The ADA and similar laws in states such as California prohibit discrimination against disabled persons in employment, specifically including HIV-positive persons. Discrimination includes the dismissal or transfer of an employee from a desired position if he or she is able or qualified to perform the duties of that position or there is some form of "reasonable accommodation" that the employer can provide to permit the employee to perform those duties without incurring extreme financial or operational hardship to the employer.

While the ADA permits an employer to discriminate if the disabled employee would pose a "significant risk to the health and safety of others" when serving in the desired position, case law interpreting the term *significant risk* provides that whether an employee poses a significant risk depends largely upon the nature of the risk and the probability that, if the risk is a disease, it will be transmitted under the particular conditions of the employee's job. [*School Board of Nassau County v. Arline,* 107 S.Ct. 1123 (1987).] In evaluating whether a person poses a significant risk, courts are to defer to the "reasoned medical judgments" of "public health officials." [*Id.*] Generally, courts applying this analysis in the case of HIV-positive persons have refused to legitimize the possible fear that an HIV-positive person will arouse in fellow employees or customers. These courts have held that an HIV-positive person working in a non-health-related occupation, such as teaching, will not pose a significant risk.

Even employees in health care fields may not be held to pose a significant risk that would justify their dismissal or transfer from the job, although this question has not been resolved definitively by the courts. In the case of an HIV-positive health care employee, resolution of the question whether such person could be transferred or otherwise limited in job duties will likely turn on expert medical judgments of public health officials, for example, the CDC.

The CDC recommends that HIV-infected health care workers be permitted to continue performing invasive procedures that are not "exposure-prone," provided CDC-recommended infection control techniques are observed. The CDC's definition of "exposure-prone" procedures covers those that involve "digital palpation of a needle tip in a body cavity or the simultaneous presence of [the worker's hand] and a . . . sharp . . . in a poorly visualized or highly confined anatomic site." [See "Recommendations for Preventing Transmission of Human Immunodeficiency Virus and Hepatitis B Virus to Patients during Exposure-Prone Invasive Procedures," *Morbidity and Mortality Weekly Report* (July 12, 1991).] Congress has enacted a law requiring states to implement these recommendations. [Treasury Appropriations Act, P.L. 102-141, Section 633 (Oct. 28, 1991)]

In short, in most situations, an employer would probably not be permitted under the ADA to impose restrictions on the job duties of an HIV-positive person, even a health care worker, unless that person was performing "exposure-prone" invasive procedures.

Q.9:26 Have there been any administrative or court cases in which a health care employer attempted to impose duty restrictions on an HIV-positive person?

Yes. A good example is the case of *Westchester County Medical Center*. In *In the Matter of Westchester County Medical Center, Department of Health and Human Services Civil Rights Reviewing*

Authority, No. 91-504-2, DAB Decision No. 1357 (September 25, 1992), HHS sued a hospital for allegedly discriminating against an HIV-positive pharmacist in violation of the Rehabilitation Act. In that case, the hospital denied the infected pharmacist's application for a particular job on the basis of a policy prohibiting the assignment of "actively infected" persons to jobs that encompassed certain tasks, including handling parenteral products.

The specific job for which the pharmacist had applied involved rotating through positions in several pharmacies operated by the medical center and filling prescriptions for parenteral products, a task that required using needles and syringes to transfer substances from one container to another. While denying the pharmacist's application for this particular job, the medical center did offer him employment in a more limited post, where he would work at a single pharmacy and would not fill prescriptions for parenteral products.

The medical center argued that a key reason for offering the HIV-positive pharmacist such limited employment was the concern that, without such limitations, the pharmacist might transmit HIV to a patient through contamination of a parenteral product with his own blood as a result of a needlestick accident. Consequently, patients of the medical center who received such contaminated parenteral products would be exposed to HIV. This prospect, according to the medical center, constituted a "direct threat" (i.e., a "significant risk") to the health and safety of others.

The Administrative Law Judge (ALJ) who rendered the first of two decisions in the case considered at length the medical center's argument that the pharmacist presented a "direct threat" to others. Evaluating this argument, the ALJ applied the "significant risk" analysis of *Arline*, focusing on the fourth element of the *Arline* test, the probability that a communicable disease would be transmitted and would cause varying degrees of harm. The ALJ framed his analysis by stating, "I would find a 'direct threat' or 'significant risk' . . . if there was even a *slight measurable risk* that Doe might infect patients through his preparation of parenteral products." (Emphasis added.) *[In the Matter of Westchester County Medical Center, Department of Health and Human Services Civil Rights*

Reviewing Authority, No. 91-504-2, DAB Decision No. 1357 (Sept. 25, 1992) (hereinafter, "CRRA Decision") at 19, quoting *In the Matter of Westchester County Medical Center*, No. 91-504-2, DAB Decision No. 191 (April 20, 1992) (hereinafter, "ALJ Decision") at 47]

The ALJ's consideration of the "significant risk" issue involved evaluating arguments and evidence bearing on the possibility that HIV might be transmitted to patients under the conditions involved in the pharmacist's desired position. The medical center contended that there was a measurable risk that the pharmacist could infect patients with HIV, under the following scenario:

> During the course of preparing a parenteral product, [the pharmacist] might, without being aware that he had done so, prick himself with one of the needles he used to transfer substances from one container to another. [He] might then use that needle, contaminated with his blood, to transfer substances between containers. That act would transfer [the pharmacist's] blood (and HIV) to a container holding a parenteral product to be administered to a patient. Ultimately, the contaminated parenteral product would be administered to a patient, and the patient might become infected by the HIV present in the product. [CRRA Decision at 21, quoting ALJ Decision at 42-43]

On the other hand, the government relied on studies by the CDC of the transmission of HIV and HBV, citing specific findings by the CDC that no incidence of HIV transmission or HBV by a pharmacist to a patient through a contaminated parenteral product has ever been documented. The government also placed in evidence a CDC finding that the risk of transmission of HIV or HBV by infected health care workers was limited to exposure-prone invasive procedures, that is, procedures involving invasion of body cavities where the area being worked on is difficult to visualize and where sharp instruments are involved.

Considering these points, the ALJ found that the preparation of parenteral products does not meet the CDC's criteria for exposure-prone invasive procedures.

The ALJ also found that the scenario proffered by the medical center constituted "speculation about a possible chain of events, without proof that there is a likelihood that the events . . . would or even could occur." [CRRA Decision at 21, quoting ALJ Decision at 42] In making this determination, the ALJ analyzed exhaustively the prospects that the scenario posited by the medical center might happen.

First, he found that, while pharmacists occasionally do sustain needlesticks in preparing parenteral products, the medical center failed to establish any likelihood that a pharmacist would injure himself or herself with a needle without being aware of the accident. Instead, the ALJ noted evidence in the record that parenteral products are prepared with the pharmacist's hands in full view, and that standard aseptic technique requires the pharmacist to avoid any contact with the needle. Thus, the ALJ reasoned, it was reasonable to conclude that a diligent pharmacist would be able to notice any needlestick he or she incurred.

Further, the ALJ noted testimony by Health and Human Services (HHS) witnesses that, in their experience, no needlestick accidents had occurred in pharmacies. Although witnesses for the hospital testified that unrecognized needlesticks did occur in pharmacies, the ALJ pointed out that such testimony was supported only by personal anecdotes. Additionally, the ALJ found that there were no studies showing that unrecognized needlesticks happened with any meaningful frequency. As for evidence in the record that episodes of unnoticed self-injury incurred by surgeons have been documented, the ALJ discounted this evidence as irrelevant because there may be poor visualization in the case of surgical procedures, leading to unnoticed needlesticks, but not in the preparation of parenteral products.

In addition to discounting the possibility that a pharmacist could incur an unnoticed needlestick, the ALJ went on to note that for such needlestick to result in the transmission of HIV to parenteral products would require the needle to be contaminated with blood containing an *infectious* dose of HIV, and the blood would have to be transmitted from the needle to the parenteral product. With regard to the first possibility, the ALJ rejected the medical center's argument that there was evidence that even a small quantity of HIV-infected blood was sufficient to cause infection. The ALJ pointed out that a journal article cited by the medical center had in fact stated that a single, small inoculum of blood delivered parenterally is associated with a very *low* risk of infection.

As to the second possibility, the ALJ concluded that the presence of protective barriers in many situations in which needles are used to transfer substances between containers reduced the likelihood of blood being transmitted from the needle to the parenteral product. Finally, the ALJ pointed out that, in order for patients to become infected with HIV in parenteral products, the virus would have to survive in such products long enough for patients to ingest them. The ALJ noted that HIV does not survive long in media other than human tissues or tissue products and that many parenteral products are toxic substances. Thus, the ALJ concluded that the argument that HIV could survive long enough in parenteral products to infect patients was mere speculation.

In short, on the discrimination issue, the ALJ concluded that the medical center had failed to establish that an unnoticed needlestick, combined with contamination of that needle with HIV-infected blood, combined with transmission of that blood from the needle into parenteral products, had even a low probability of occurring. Consequently, the HIV-positive pharmacist did not constitute a "direct threat" to patients that would prevent him from being qualified to perform the desired phlebotomist position, notwithstanding his infection with HIV. Because the pharmacist did not pose such a "direct threat" to patients, the ALJ concluded that the medical center had discriminated against him in violation of the Rehabilitation Act by offering him only a restricted pharmacy position instead of the broader position that he desired and for which he had applied. In reviewing the ALJ's decision, the CRRA considered in detail the arguments of the parties and the related evidence on the record, concluding that the evidence supported the findings and conclusions of the ALJ.

The CRRA summarized its conclusions as follows:

> In summary, we conclude that Westchester did not rebut DHHS's *prima facie* case that [the pharmacist] does not

> pose a direct threat of communicating his HIV infection to others in the course of preparing parenteral products. Westchester merely posited that a long sequence of highly unlikely events would occur, overcoming many potentially critical supervening factors such as aseptic technique, the use of protective barriers, dissolution or destruction of the virus in the parenteral product, and storage of the products under unknown conditions, as well as the demonstrated low risk of infection even among those receiving direct needlesticks. Westchester did not establish that any of the individual events in its scenario had even an extremely low probability of occurring or that the entire chain of events was more than a speculative hypothetical. We therefore conclude that there is substantial evidence in the record to support the ALJ's determination that [the pharmacist] does not pose a direct threat on this basis. [CRRA Decision at 30]

With respect to the remedy for the medical center's discrimination, the ALJ concluded that terminating all federal financial assistance (i.e., all Medicare and Medicaid payments) to the medical center would be appropriate. While noting that Rehabilitation Act regulations state that such action must be limited to the particular program or part of a program in which noncompliance has been found, the ALJ also pointed out that the medical center's action with respect to the pharmacist was based on a *general policy* of discriminating against HIV-infected employees, and that policy affected all medical center programs receiving Medicare/Medicaid payments.

The medical center argued that it did not have a policy of discriminating against HIV-infected employees, contending that its policy simply prohibited pharmacists who are "actively infected" with any communicable disease from handling intravenous fluids, and that the policy clearly was not HIV-specific because it predated the discovery of the virus. However, the ALJ rejected this argument, observing that as long as the medical center claimed that it acted reasonably in the case of the pharmacist, the potential for it to "impose similarly arbitrary restrictions against any HIV-infected employee or job applicant" continued to exist. [CRRA Decision at 37, quoting ALJ Decision at 54]

In reviewing the ALJ's decision on the remedy, CRRA agreed with his reasoning. The CRRA added that, even if the medical center's discriminatory policy was limited to the pharmacist, terminating all Medicare and Medicaid funding was reasonable because the funds "used to support [the medical center's] discrimination against [the pharmacist]" were commingled with other funds to support the medical center's entire operation. (Subsequently, however, the medical center avoided the termination by agreeing to a settlement under which the pharmacist would be offered the desired job and given about $300,000 in back pay and costs.)

Q.9:27 Do principles of medical ethics address AIDS-related issues?

Yes. The AMA has issued a number of pronouncements on AIDS-related issues. As noted previously, Opinion 9.131 of the AMA's 1992 *Code of Medical Ethics Current Opinions* provides that a physician may not ethically refuse to treat a patient whose condition is within his or her practice area solely because the patient is HIV-positive. The same opinion addresses actions to be taken by a physician who knows that he or she is HIV-positive:

> A physician who knows that he or she is seropositive [for HIV] should not engage in any activity that creates a risk of transmission of the disease to others. A physician who has HIV disease or who is seropositive should consult colleagues as to which activities the physician can pursue without creating a risk to patients. [AMA, Council on Ethical and Judicial Affairs, *Code of Medical Ethics Current Opinions*, Opinion No. 9.131 (1992).]

Additionally, the AMA's *Policy Compendium* of the House of Delegates (1991) includes numerous AIDS-related opinions. These opinions address, among other things, the following:

- The classification of AIDS as a communicable and sexually transmitted disease;
- Consent required for HIV testing;
- HIV-infection reporting;
- Disability insurance for HIV- and HBV-infected health care workers;
- HIV home test kits;
- Reporting and follow-up on HIV-positive persons;
- Education for health care professionals on HIV and AIDS;
- The ethical responsibility of a physician to treat HIV-positive persons;
- Education of prospective blood donors about the safety of blood donation and blood transfusion;
- Education of physicians on alternatives to blood transfusions;
- Appropriateness of limitations on the duties of HIV-positive health care workers; and
- The availability of, and procedures for, HIV testing.

With regard to availability and procedures for HIV testing, the *Policy Compendium* provides as follows:

> *HIV Testing Availability* (17a) continues to recommend that HIV testing be readily available to all who wish to be tested, including having available sites for confidential testing; (17b) encourages persons who suspect that they have been exposed to HIV to be tested so that appropriate treatment and counseling can begin for those who are seropositive; (17c) encourages physicians and laboratories to review their procedures to assure that HIV testing conforms to standards that will produce the highest level of accuracy; (17d) supports considering an award recognition program for physicians who donate a portion of their professional time to testing and counseling those patients who could not otherwise afford services;
>
> *Testing Procedures* (18a) recommends that appropriate medical organizations establish rigorous proficiency test-

ing and quality control procedures for testing laboratories on a frequent and regular basis. [American Medical Association House of Delegates, *Policy Compendium* (1991) at 20.966]

10

Drug Testing

Q.10:1 What is the estimated prevalence of drug use on the job?

Studies conducted by various sources (including the Bureau of Labor Statistics and the National Drug Control Strategy for the Workplace) during the late 1980s indicated that generally, 10 percent to 20 percent of American workers used illegal drugs on the job or tested positive for illegal drugs in a job-application–related drug test. Statistics compiled by the National Institute on Drug Abuse (NIDA) estimated that, in 1990, 14 percent to 15 percent of workers would test positive.

Q.10:2 What are the purposes of drug testing?

Generally, the purposes of drug testing are to reduce or eliminate the costs associated with on-the-job drug use or drug-related impairment. Recent NIDA data show, for example, that drug users have the following:

- Three and one half times more on-the-job accidents,
- More frequent and longer absences from work,
- Five times more Workers Compensation claims,
- Three times more sickness benefits,
- Three times more lateness, and
- Over two times more time off from work than non-drug–users.

Of 681 drug-testing firms recently surveyed, 77% cited better quality applicants, 63% greater workplace safety, 58% improved image in the community, 56% fewer direct drug-related problems, and 54% improved morale following the institution of drug-testing programs.

Perhaps for these reasons, the frequency of drug-testing programs among Fortune 500 companies rose from 3% in 1983 to 80% in 1990.

Q.10:3 What substances are typically identified in workplace drug testing?

The substances typically identified in workplace drug testing are the following:

- Marijuana,
- Cocaine,
- Opiates,
- Barbiturates,
- Amphetamines,
- Phencyclidine hydrochloride (PCP), and
- (In about half of testing programs) alcohol.

Q.10:4 What are the types of drug testing?

The types of drug testing are as follows:

- Preemployment (application);
- Periodic, planned testing;
- Random testing;
- Postaccident testing;
- Testing based on "reasonable cause"; and
- Testing upon a return to duty after drug rehabilitation.

These types of testing may be used singly or in combination in any given workplace drug-testing program. For example, a company may test all job applicants or persons who have been offered a job and also test current employees on a periodic or random basis, as well as testing employees who have been involved in workplace accidents. The types of testing may also vary with particular job classifications.

Q.10:5 What bodily substances are typically tested for drugs?

The bodily fluids used for drug testing are blood, urine, and to some extent, saliva. Urine is the most commonly used testing substance.

Q.10:6 What does drug testing measure?

Drug testing measures the presence of drug-related metabolites, or enzymes into which drugs metabolize, rather than level of drugs themselves.

Q.10:7 What are the key measures in the drug-testing process?

The key measures in the drug-testing process are the *detection level* and the *decision*, or *cut-off, level*. The detection level is the lowest concentration of a drug that can be detected reliably by a testing method. The decision or cut-off level is the level at which a test result will be labeled *positive* or *negative*.

Q.10:8 What are the key limitations of the drug-testing process and the information it yields?

Important limitations of the drug-testing process are as follows. First, because only metabolites, rather than drugs themselves, are measured, it is impossible to infer from the testing results either the time when the drug was ingested or the size of the dose.

Second, detection periods (the latest point following ingestion at which the drug can be detected by a testing method) vary depending on the properties of the particular drug, the physical characteristics of the user, and the user's history of drug use. For example, detection periods range from only 12 to 18 hours for cocaine, to 2 to 7 days for casual use of marijuana, and over 1 month for regular use of marijuana. Because of these limitations, the results of drug tests cannot be used to assess whether the person tested is currently impaired and cannot identify the degree of risk associated with that employee's continuing to work.

Q.10:9 What are the constitutional limitations on drug testing?

Constitutional issues surrounding drug testing generally arise with regard to the testing of public-sector or publicly regulated employees, because the government-related nature of the job raises the issue of whether a drug test constitutes an unreasonable governmental search and seizure in violation of the Fourth Amendment to the United States Constitution.

The constitutionality of drug testing varies with the type of testing. Postaccident testing of railroad workers was upheld by the United States Supreme Court in *Skinner v. National Railway Executives Association*, 109 S.Ct. 1402 (1989), upholding Federal Railroad Administration regulations mandating postaccident breath and urine tests of railroad workers without "individualized suspicion" or warrant, on the grounds that the purpose of testing was related to the special need to prevent railway accidents and the relatively small amount of intrusion into personal privacy involved in the particular type of testing. The Supreme Court upheld mandatory testing of Customs Service employees who applied for promotion to jobs involving drug enforcement or carrying of firearms in *National Treasury Employees Union v. Von Raab*, 109 S.Ct. 1384 (1989), for reasons similar to those in the *Skinner* case. However, the court in *Von Raab* remanded the case to a lower court for further determinations as to the constitutionality of drug testing for employees seeking promotion to jobs that did not entail drug enforcement or carrying of firearms, but merely handling of classified materials.

Essentially, in the *Skinner* and *Von Raab* cases, the Supreme Court formulated a balancing test that balances the degree of governmental interest or public safety concerns implicated in drug testing against the degree of intrusion into employee privacy involved in the particular type of drug-testing program.

In applying such a balancing analysis, most courts have upheld the constitutionality of preemployment testing on the grounds that the applicant is free to choose whether to take the test or to withdraw the application without consequence, and thus, there is a minimal invasion of privacy.

When public safety is involved, courts have generally upheld the constitutionality of periodic testing. Similarly, most courts have upheld the constitutionality of random testing when it is related to "safety-sensitive" positions. The Supreme Court has suggested that random testing in safety-sensitive positions may be constitutional by denying *certiorari* in two cases: (1) *Policeman's Benevolent Association v. Township of Washington*, 850 F.2d 133 (2d Cir.), *cert. denied*, No. 88-706 (U.S. Apr. 1988), upholding random testing of police officers; (2) *Alvarado v. Washington Public Power Supply System*, 759 P.2d 427 (Wash.), *cert. denied*, No. 88-645 (U.S. Apr. 1988), upholding a random testing program for employees at nuclear power plants.

Finally, courts have not addressed return-to-duty testing, but would probably uphold its constitutionality on grounds related to those described above.

In the private sector, constitutional issues are not implicated by drug testing, except in those states the constitutions of which include explicit privacy guarantees (e.g., California and Florida). Challenges to drug testing programs in those states have applied analyses similar to that of the U.S. Supreme Court, balancing the governmental or safety interests further by a drug-testing program against the degree of intrusion into employee privacy involved.

Q.10:10 What legal issues are raised by drug testing in the private sector?

Some of the legal issues implicated by drug testing in the private sector are as follows:

- **Defamation:** An employee about whom false information concerning drug testing was made public and who suffered injury to reputation or character as a result could sue for defamation.
- **Infliction of emotional distress:** A person who suffered very severe emotional distress due to improper action during the drug testing process could sue to recover. (For example, in one case, an employee won a judgment of $125,000 due to the extraordinary discomfort caused by direct observation of the urination process during the collection of a drug testing sample.)
- **Invasion of privacy:** An employee whose test result was improperly disclosed by the employer or who, in the drug-testing process, suffered some form of "outrageous contact" could sue for damages.
- **Breach of contract:** An employee might be able to sue for breach of contract in a case where the actual drug-testing process in which he or she was involved in some way violated the employer's stated drug-testing policies or procedures.

Q.10:11 Who regulates drug testing?

State, federal, and some local governments regulate workplace drug testing.

Q.10:12 How do states regulate drug testing?

Various states have enacted statutes that regulate the circumstances under which employers may institute drug-testing programs, prescribe the rights of employees subjected to such testing programs, and, in some cases, establish limitations on the disclosure of drug-testing results.

Among those states and localities that have enacted drug-testing statutes are the following:

- Berkeley, California;
- San Francisco, California;

- Boulder, Colorado;
- Connecticut;
- Florida;
- Iowa;
- Louisiana;
- Maine;
- Minnesota;
- Montana;
- Nebraska;
- Oregon;
- Rhode Island,
- Utah; and
- Vermont.

These statutes vary in the degree to which they encourage or restrict drug testing.

Q.10:13 Do any states require drug testing to be performed by specifically licensed laboratories?

Some states require employers conducting testing to use laboratories that are specifically licensed to perform drug tests. Among these states are Maryland, Nebraska, and Oregon. [See Md. Ann. Code §17-214.1 (1988); Neb. Rev. Stat. §48-19-01-10 (1988); Oreg. Rev. Stat. §438.510 (1987).]

Q.10:14 What aspects of the testing process are typically affected by state laws?

As noted above, state laws vary in breadth, specificity, and the degree to which they encourage or limit drug testing. The most comprehensive statutes may address the following:

- The circumstances in which employers may require drug or alcohol testing;

- Requirements for a workplace drug and alcohol testing policy;
- Notice and consent requirements for drug testing;
- Use of licensed laboratories;
- Procedures for chain of custody protection and confirmatory testing;
- Sanctions employers may apply to persons who test positive;
- Employee rights to rehabilitation before discharge;
- Disclosure of drug-testing results; and
- Remedies for employees whose rights under the statute have been infringed.

Less comprehensive laws simply limit the circumstances under which employers can test for drugs or the types of testing that may be conducted.

Q.10:15 Do any jurisdictions ban drug testing?

At least one jurisdiction bans drug testing. Berkeley, California, passed a resolution in 1988 that imposed an absolute ban on drug testing of employees or applicants within city borders.

Q.10:16 What is an example of a comprehensive state drug-testing law?

One example of such a law is Minnesota's drug testing statute. This law imposes the following conditions on workplace drug testing:

- **Limitations on circumstances when drug testing can be conducted:** Employers can require preemployment testing only if the job has already been offered, and all applicants are tested; employers may require testing as part of a routine physical only if it is done once a year, and employees are given two weeks written notice of the testing; random testing is limited to safety-sensitive jobs; reasonable-suspicion testing may be conducted only on suspicion of current drug or alcohol impairment, a drug-related work rule violation, or involvement of the employee in an injury or accident; and testing in connection with a treatment program, without notice, can only be conducted during the pendency of the program or within two years after its completion.

- **Policy statement:** An explicit *policy statement* that says employers have no duty to test employees for drugs.
- **Written policy:** Employers who conduct drug testing must have a written policy that states who will be tested, when testing will be done, the consequences of refusing to be tested or receiving a positive result, employee rights to have a retest at their own expense and to explain positive results, and any appeal procedures provided.
- **Testing notice requirements:** Notice must be provided to all workers as soon as the employer adopts a drug-testing policy, an employee must receive notice of the drug-testing policy upon transfer to an affected job, notice must be provided to applicants when they are hired and before they are tested, notice of the policy must be posted, and copies must be available.
- **Consent requirements:** There must be a consent form in which the employee acknowledges the drug-testing policy and has an opportunity to identify medications he or she is taking and any other information relevant to drug testing.
- **Laboratory testing requirements:** Testing must be done by a licensed laboratory, which must adhere to the state requirements, follow a specified chain of custody procedure, and perform a confirmatory test.
- **Sanctions:** Employees may not be discharged after the first positive result on a drug test without being given the opportunity for rehabilitation, but an employee may be suspended after an initial positive result when suspension is necessary to protect other employees or the public.
- **Confidentiality protection:** The testing laboratory may disclose to the employer only results relating to the presence or absence of drugs or their metabolites; employers and laboratories may not disclose drug-testing results to a third party without the employee's consent.

- **Employee remedies:** Employees who suffer a violation of the Minnesota drug-testing requirements may sue for damages and attorney's fees or injunctive or other equitable relief. Employers are prohibited from retaliating against employees who avail themselves of these remedies.

Q.10:17 How does the federal government regulate drug testing?

At the federal level, drug testing was initially regulated by Executive Order 12564, 51 Fed. Reg. 32889 (March 28, 1986), which required each executive department and agency of the United States government to develop a plan for achieving the objective of a drug-free workplace, including measures such as testing to identify illegal drug users. Under this executive order, the Secretary of Health and Human Services (HHS) was authorized to promulgate scientific and technical guidelines to govern federal agencies' drug-testing programs. Pursuant to this authority, the National Institute on Drug Abuse (NIDA) promulgated an extensive scientific and technical program regulating the process of drug testing. [51 Fed. Reg. 11970 (Apr. 11, 1988)] In addition to the scientific and technical standards contained in these NIDA regulations, those federal agencies that have established drug-testing programs have promulgated regulations concerning drug testing of their own employees and drug testing required by private-sector employers with which the agencies have contracts.

In addition to requiring federal agencies to establish drug-testing programs, the federal government also imposes drug-testing requirements on certain federal contractors. Pursuant to the Drug Free Workplace Act of 1988, 41 U.S.C. §§701–707, contractors providing property or services valued at $25,000 or more and recipients of grants of any amount from any federal agency must certify to the federal government that they maintain drug-free workplaces. [41 U.S.C. §701(a)(1); 48 C.F.R. §§23.501, 23.504–505, 52.223-5] The requirements of this law apply to every site where the employee will perform work under the contract, but only to employees directly engaged in contract work. [42 U.S.C. §706(1)(2); 48 C.F.R. §23.503] The law also provides that contractors must agree not to engage in the unlawful manufacture, distribution, dispensing, possession, or use of a controlled substance in the performance of a covered contract. [48 C.F.R. §§23.504(b), 52.223-5(c), 52.223-6(c)] The federal law does not apply, however, to subcontractors of affected contractors.

Although the Act requires subject companies to establish drug-free awareness programs to inform employees about the dangers of drug abuse in the workplace and the particular employer's drug-free workplace policy, it does not expressly require drug testing, rehabilitation, or any particular personnel actions against persons working under the influence of drugs. Instead, the Act provides that a contractor can be subject to suspension of payments, contract termination, or debarment if the contractor fails to comply with the specific requirements of the Act or has such a large number of employees convicted of criminal drug violations in the workplace as to indicate that the contractor has failed to make a good-faith effort to provide a drug-free workplace. [41 U.S.C. §§701(b)(1), 704; 48 C.F.R. §§9.406-1(c), 9.406-2(c), 9.407-1(d), 9.407-2(a)(4), 23.506]

Q.10:18 What aspects of the testing process do the NIDA regulations affect?

Generally, the NIDA regulations establish extremely detailed standards for the technical aspects of the drug-testing process. The regulations provide that only NIDA-certified laboratories will be permitted to perform drug testing for federal agencies or contractors with federal agencies, and establish criteria for the certification of such laboratories. The regulations specify the substances for which federal employees or employees of federal contractors may be tested, making testing for marijuana and cocaine mandatory and testing for opiates, amphetamines, PCP, and other controlled substances permissive, and requiring HHS permission for testing for drugs not listed on federal Schedules I and II of controlled substances. The certification standards for drug testing laboratories include extensive requirements as to aspects of the laboratory drug-testing process.

Q.10:19 How do the NIDA regulations relate to CLIA'88?

Laboratories certified by NIDA to perform drug testing for federal agencies or contractors are exempt from CLIA'88.

Q.10:20 How do the NIDA regulations differ from CLIA'88?

While both sets of regulations include detailed requirements for testing personnel and the testing process, there are key differences between the CLIA'88 requirements (which all laboratories in the United States, regardless of their testing menus, must observe) and the NIDA regulations. These key, distinguishing features include the following:

- The NIDA regulations include special chain of custody procedures for specimen collection and for handling of specimens during testing and storage.
- The NIDA regulations include stringent standards for making the site of drug testing secure, for restricting access to all but authorized personnel, and for providing an escort for any other people who are authorized to be on the premises.
- The NIDA regulations include performance testing requirements specific to urine assays for the presence of illegal drugs.
- The NIDA regulations contain specific educational and experience requirements for laboratory personnel to ensure their competence and credibility as experts in forensic urine drug testing, particularly to qualify them as witnesses in legal proceedings that challenge laboratory findings on drug tests.

Q.10:21 Do the NIDA regulations apply to drug testing of persons under the jurisdiction of the criminal justice system, such as prisoners, parolees, and so forth?

No. According to NIDA, testing of persons in the criminal justice system differs from testing under the authority of Executive Order 12564 because the legal issues at issue in the criminal justice system are different from those in civil drug testing, and the incidence of drug testing among prisoners is different from that in the workplace or other civil arenas.

Q.10:22 Do the NIDA regulations apply to military testing of service personnel or applicants for the uniformed services?

No.

Q.10:23 Do the NIDA guidelines apply to federal contract employees?

No. However, any agency may require any of its contractors to test its own employees, using the procedures in the NIDA guidelines, by making such testing requirement a term or condition of the contract.

Q.10:24 Generally, what do the NIDA regulations do?

The NIDA regulations establish a certification program and certification for standards for clinical laboratories that wish to perform drug testing for federal agencies and employees of certain federal contractors pursuant to Executive Order 12564. To perform drug testing for such entities, a clinical laboratory must receive NIDA certification and, consequently, must satisfy the standards in the NIDA regulations.

Q.10:25 What drugs are addressed by the NIDA certification program?

To be certified by NIDA, a clinical laboratory must be capable of testing for at least the following five classes of drugs: (1) marijuana, (2) cocaine, (3) opiates, (4) amphetamines, and (5) phencyclidine.

The NIDA certification program is limited to these classes of drugs, and the laboratory will be surveyed and performance tested only for these drugs and specific methods for testing for them. NIDA certification of a laboratory thus indicates that any test result that the laboratory reports for an entity of the federal government meets the standards of the NIDA regulations for the five classes of drugs using the methods specified.

Q.10:26 How do the NIDA regulations address initial and confirmatory testing?

The NIDA regulations require that a drug-testing laboratory have the capability of performing both initial immunoassays and confirmatory gas chromatography/mass spectrometry (GC/MS) tests for the five classes of drugs identified above, and for any other drug or metabolite for which agency drug testing is authorized, at the same site. The regulations further require that all positive initial test results be confirmed before they are reported.

Q.10:27 Do the NIDA regulations contain any unique requirements concerning specimen collection?

Yes. The NIDA regulations include detailed requirements for specimen collection, most notably certain minimum precautions that are intended to ensure that unadulterated specimens are obtained and correctly identified. These precautions are as follows:

- **Deterring specimen dilution:** To deter dilution of specimens at the collection site, the laboratory must place toilet bluing agents in toilet tanks whenever possible, so that the water in the toilet bowl is always blue. There should be no other source of water, such as a shower or sink, within the enclosure where urination occurs to produce the specimen.
- **Obtaining subject identification:** The laboratory employee at the collection site must ask each individual who arrives to furnish a sample to present photo identification. If the drug-

test subject does not have such identification, the collection-site employee must contact his or her supervisor or another federal agency official who can positively identify the person. The collection-site employee must not proceed with this collection of the specimen until or unless the drug-test subject is positively identified.

- **Removing personal belongings:** The collection-site employee must ask the drug-test subject to remove any outergarments, such as a coat or jacket, that might conceal items or substances that can be used to tamper with the urine specimen. The collection-site employee must also ensure that the drug-test subject's personal belongings, such as a purse or briefcase, remain with the outergarments, away from the subject during the collection process.
- **Supervised handwashing:** The drug-test subject must be instructed to wash and dry his or her hands before giving the sample. After washing the hands, the drug-test subject must remain in the presence of the collection-site employee and not have access to any water fountain, water faucet, soap dispenser, cleaning agent, or any other materials that might be used to tamper with the specimen.
- **Noting unusual behavior:** The drug-test subject may provide the specimen in the privacy of a stall or partitioned area, but the collection-site employee must note any unusual behavior or appearance of the drug-test subject in the laboratory's permanent recordbook.
- **Ensuring adequate sample size:** If the specimen contains less than 60 mL of urine, the collection-site employee must ask for a second sample to allow the total specimen to reach 60 mL.
- **Measuring specimen temperature:** Immediately after the collection of the specimen, the collection-site employee must measure the specimen's temperature. No more than four minutes may elapse from the time of urination to the measurement of the temperature. The purpose of this temperature measurement is to determine whether the individual may have altered or substituted a specimen. If the temperature of the specimen is outside a range prescribed in the regulations, then another

sample must be collected under direct observation of the test subject by a collection-site employee of the same gender. Both specimens must then be forwarded to the laboratory for testing.

- **Inspecting the specimen:** Immediately after collection of the specimen, the collection-site employee must also inspect the specimen to determine its color and look for any unusual signs, and must note any unusual findings in the permanent recordbook. Whenever there is any reason to believe that the specimen has been altered or adulterated, a second specimen must be obtained as soon as possible under the direct observation of a same-gender collection-site employee.
- **Keeping the specimen in view:** The drug-test subject and the collection-site employee must keep the specimen in view at all times before it is sealed and labeled.
- **Labeling the specimen:** The collection-site employee must securely place on the collection bottle an identification label including the date, the individual's specimen number, and any other identifying information provided or required by the federal agency. The drug-test subject must initial the identification label in order to certify that it is his or her specimen. The collection-site employee must enter in the permanent recordbook all information identifying the specimen and must sign the book next to this information.
- **Obtaining test subject certification:** The drug-test subject must be asked to read and sign a statement in the permanent recordbooks certifying that the specimen identified as his or hers is in fact the specimen he or she provided.
- **Chain of custody form:** The collection-site person must complete the chain of custody form before shipping the specimen for testing.

Q.10:28 Do the NIDA regulations contain any specific requirements for reporting of test results?

Yes. The NIDA regulations impose the following requirements concerning reporting of test results:

- The drug-testing laboratory must report test results to the agency's medical review officer within an average of five working days following the laboratory's receipt of the drug-testing specimen.

- Before any test result is reported, it must be reviewed and the test certified as an accurate report by the individual responsible for the overall operation of the laboratory.

- The drug-testing report must identify the drugs/metabolites tested for, the cutoff for each, whether the result was positive or negative, the specimen number assigned by the agency, and the drug-testing laboratory specimen identification number.

- Only specimens that are confirmed positive (i.e., those that are positive on both the initial and the confirmatory test) may be reported positive for a specific drug.

- The agency medical review officer may request the laboratory to quantify test results, and the laboratory must provide such quantification.

- Test results may be transmitted by fax or other electronic means, but may not be reported verbally by telephone. The laboratory must ensure the security of the data transmission method and must limit access to any data transmission, storage, and retrieval system.

- The testing laboratory must send to the medical review officer only a certified copy of the original chain of custody forms signed by the individual responsible for the day-to-day management of the testing laboratory or the individual responsible for attesting to the validity reports.

- The testing laboratory must provide to the agency official who is responsible for coordination of the agency drug-free workplace program a monthly statistical summary of drug testing on federal employees. The summary must contain certain items of information specified in the regulations.

Q.10:29 What actions might put a laboratory at risk for negligence liability in the drug-testing process?

Failure to observe professional standards in any aspect of the drug-testing process—such as chain of custody, calibration of equipment, reporting of results, and so forth—could put a laboratory at risk for negligence liability if such misconduct caused an erroneously positive drug-test report and resulted in injury to the test subject. In states that have imposed statutory limitations on disclosure of drug-test results, failure to observe such restrictions might expose the laboratory to risk of liability if harm to the test subject resulted.

11

The Laboratory As Employer

Q.11:1 What activities conducted by the laboratory in its role as an employer are subject to regulation?

The principal activities conducted by the laboratory in its role as employer that are subject to regulation are employee relations activities (hiring, firing, compensation, and similar decisions) as well as activities affecting the organization of labor unions and the management of facilities and equipment in the workplace that affect overall occupational safety and health.

Q.11:2 Who regulates such conduct?

Such activities are regulated principally by the federal government through various labor, antidiscrimination, and occupational safety and health laws. However, some states also regulate labor relations, workplace discrimination, and workplace safety and health.

Q.11:3 What major federal laws affect labor relations and labor standards?

The major laws affecting labor relations are the National Labor Relations Act (NLRA) and the Fair Labor Standards Act (FLSA). The NLRA establishes the rights of employers, employees, and unions in relation to the collective bargaining process. Although there are numerous state labor relations laws, the NLRA will generally predominate under the doctrine of federal preemption.

The FLSA deals with wages, hours, and working conditions. Although many states have labor standards, the FLSA dominates this area.

Q.11:4 Which federal agencies or departments administer the federal labor relations laws?

The NLRA is administered by the National Labor Relations Board, an independent agency consisting of two parts: (1) a board of five members, who decide unfair labor practices and representation cases, and (2) a general counsel's office, which acts as investigator and prosecutor of charges of unfair labor practices. The FLSA is administered by the Department of Labor.

Q.11:5 What does the NLRA regulate?

The NLRA, 29 U.S.C. §151 *et seq.*, regulates collective bargaining. The purpose of the NLRA is to protect interstate commerce by fostering proper operation of the collective bargaining process. The law seeks to accomplish this purpose by defining the rights of employers and employees, protecting the right of employees to organize and select collective bargaining representatives, and identifying and proscribing as "unfair labor practices" those actions on the part of labor and management that interfere with the collective bargaining process.

Q.11:6 What employer practices does the NLRA define as "unfair labor practices"?

Section 8(a) of the NLRA, 29 U.S.C. §158(a), spells out unfair labor practices on the part of the employer. These unfair labor practices are as follows:

- **Illegal interference, restraint, or coercion:** There is an umbrella provision whereby any infringement by an employer of the collective bargaining rights secured to the employee in the NLRA becomes automatically an unfair labor practice. This umbrella provision is now held specifically to prohibit threats, interrogation, surveillance, or violence on the part of the employer toward employees. (A union that fines its members for resigning from the union during a strike and returning to work is guilty of an unfair labor practice even if the union's constitution expressly prohibits such resignations, according to the U.S. Supreme Court. In *Pattern Makers' League of North America v. NLRB*, 105 S. Ct. 3064 (1985), the court upheld the NLRB's ruling that such fines constitute an unfair labor practice because they "restrain or coerce" employees in the exercise of the rights granted to them by the NLRA. In reaching its conclusion, the court adopted a distinction drawn by the NLRB between fining current union members and fining those who have resigned from the union. While the court viewed the former as noncoercive and within a union's right to control its "internal affairs," it viewed the latter as an invalid restriction on an employee's right to resign.)

- **Illegal assistance or domination:** The aim is to maintain the integrity of the collective bargaining process by keeping management and labor on opposite sides of the bargaining table. There are several employer activities held to be illegal assistance or domination: giving financial aid to the union, recognizing a union that represents only a minority of the employees, and giving preferential treatment to one union when there are two or more unions competing to represent the employees.
- **Discrimination to encourage or discourage union activity:** It is unlawful for an employer to discriminate in any way against an employee or an applicant on the basis of that person's union activity. The most frequent prohibitions that occur as a result of this provision are prohibitions against firing and blacklisting union organizers.
- **Discrimination for filing charges or giving testimony:** The aim of this prohibition is to prevent any hiring or on-the-job discrimination against the employee who brings charges or gives testimony before the NLRB or a comparable forum.

- **Refusal to bargain:** The employer may incur a charge of refusal to bargain if he or she fails to observe any of several affirmative obligations that fall to him or her as part of the collective bargaining process. For instance, the employer must exclusively recognize the union that has been duly chosen to represent the employees. Once a union has been chosen, management cannot attempt to play one union off against another. Further, the management team must bargain in good faith, a concept that is rather difficult to define and beyond the scope of this manual.

Q.11:7 What are some illustrations of the application of employer unfair labor practice provisions in health care settings?

The following cases illustrate the kinds of employer actions that may be prohibited as "unfair labor practices" in a health care setting.

The Supreme Court's landmark ruling in *Beth Israel Hospital v. NLRB*, 437 U.S. 483 (1978), arose out of a hospital's rule prohibiting such union activity as solicitation in any area of the hospital to which patients have access. Specifically, the hospital had prohibited union solicitation in a cafeteria that was used primarily by hospital employees, but to which patients and their guests also had access. The NLRB found that this broad prohibition of solicitation in any area to which patients have access is illegal. On appeal, the Supreme Court agreed with the board. See *Baylor University Medical Center v. NLRB*, 439 U.S. 9 (1978) and *NLRB v. Baptist Hospital*, 442 U.S. 773 (1979) for subsequent Supreme Court rulings on permissible union solicitation in hospitals.

NLRB v. Western Clinical Laboratory, 571 F.2d 457 (9th Cir. 1978), arose in a hospital laboratory setting. In this case, the employer took over a hospital laboratory, and the technicians in the laboratory formed a union to protect their interests. The NLRB subsequently found that the employer illegally attempted to restrain the union's activities in the following ways:

- Interrogating employees about their union sympathies;
- Threatening that collective activity of the employees would be futile;

- Threatening the job security of an employee because of his adherence to the union;
- Soliciting grievances from employees and promising correction in order to undermine adherence to the union;
- Attempting to cause another employee to fire an employee who testified in the NLRB's review of the dispute;
- Issuing poor work evaluations to three employees, and firing one of them, because of their union involvement; and
- Requiring an employee to use vacation time for part of his attendance under subpoena at the NLRB hearing.

On appeal, the Ninth Circuit upheld the NLRB. *NLRB v. Western Clinical Laboratory* is particularly informative because of its lengthy list of employer practices that, in the setting of a hospital laboratory labor dispute, are probably forbidden by the Act.

Another hospital case illustrates employer conduct that may be deemed illegal in connection with union elections. Specifically, a hospital's announcement of a wage increase for all employees only two weeks before a union representation election constitutes an unfair labor practice that interferes with employees' protected rights to organize. [*St. Francis Federation of Nurses & Health Professionals v. NLRB*, 729 F.2d 844 (D.C. Cir. 1984)] In this case, an acute-care hospital announced a 10 percent wage increase for all employees two weeks before a union election for the bargaining unit of the hospital's nonsupervisory registered nurses. The wage increase was to be implemented in November, about ten days following the election, although the hospital's normal practice was to implement wage increases every January.

Given these facts, the NLRB held and the court of appeals affirmed that, while it might have been appropriate for the hospital to grant a wage increase pursuant to regular practice in January, the timing of the November increase and its announcement in October immediately before the union election made the wage increase an unfair preelection influencing action. The board and the court relied on Section 8(a) (1) of the NLRA, which prohibits conferring employee benefits, when a union election is pending, that are for the purpose of inducing employees to vote against the union. This section of the law bars any conduct that is immediately favorable to employees, has the express purpose of impinging on their freedom of choice for or against unionization, and is reasonably calculated to have that effect.

A health care institution may also commit an unfair labor practice by interfering impermissibly with the organizational activities of its off-duty employees. In *Ohio Masonic Home*, 290 NLRB No. 122 (1988), a nursing home issued a rule prohibiting off-duty employees from entering the employer's premises to "engage in publicly hostile or adverse confrontations." The NLRB, in considering the legality of this rule, held that such "no-access" rules affecting organizational activities of off-duty employees are to be analyzed under the principles of *Tri-County Medical Center*, 222 NLRB No. 1089 (1976), in which the board held that a no-access rule concerning off-duty employees is valid only if the rule meets the following criteria:

- Limits access solely with respect to the interior of the facility and other working areas;
- Is clearly disseminated to all employees;
- Applies to off-duty employees seeking access to the facility for any purpose and not just to those employees engaging in union activities; and
- Does not deny off-duty employees entry to parking lots, gates, and other outside nonworking areas, except when justified by business reasons.

In the *Ohio Masonic* case, the board found that the employer's rule did not meet the first and third criteria of the *Tri-County* test, and the employer's business reasons were insufficient to justify the existence of the rule. Thus, the employer's maintenance and enforcement of the no-access rule violated the NLRA.

Q.11:8 What union actions (if any) does the NLRA define as "unfair labor practices"?

Originally, the NLRA defined only certain employer practices as "unfair." In 1947, this label was attached by amendment to a number of practices of employees and labor unions. The union unfair labor practices are set forth at 29 U.S.C. §158(b). They are as follows:

- **Union restraint and coercion:** This prohibition is primarily aimed at violence and threats on the picket line and certain coercive union disciplinary actions against union members.
- **Union discrimination:** A union may not cause or attempt to cause an employer to discriminate against an employee because of nonmembership in the union or lack of support for the union. A prime exception to this rule is that a union may enforce a valid union-shop clause of its collective bargaining agreement against employees who refuse to pay initiation fees or dues.
- **Union refusal to bargain:** Unions must also bargain in good faith, based on principles comparable to those applicable to employers, set forth in **Q.11:6**, above.
- **Secondary boycott:** A union may not engage in a "secondary boycott." A secondary boycott is the union practice of putting pressure, through the use of such techniques as a picket line, on a "secondary" or neutral employer that does business with a "primary" employer with which the union has a labor dispute. The union's aim is to force the secondary employer to pressure the primary employer into giving in to the union.
- **Excessive initiation fees:** The union may not artificially restrict its membership by charging arbitrarily high initiation fees.
- **Featherbedding**: In theory, the union may not seek through negotiation to protect economically superfluous jobs. In practice, this prohibition has proved very hard to enforce because of the difficulty, for the employer, of establishing that particular jobs are superfluous.
- **Organization and recognition picketing:** Except in narrowly confined circumstances, a union may not engage in picketing an employer when an object of the picketing is either to compel the employer to recognize a certain bargaining agent as the employees' representative or to persuade other employees to join one particular union.

- **"Hot cargo" agreements:** A "hot cargo" agreement is similar to a secondary boycott in that it involves union interaction with a second employer. The "hot cargo" prohibition bars a union from negotiating an agreement with a second employer in order to bring pressure on the primary employer. In a typical "hot cargo" agreement, a union that is in dispute with Employer A might try to secure Employer B's agreement not to do business with Employer A.

Q.11:9 What is an illustration of the application of union unfair labor practice provisions in health care settings?

The following case illustrates the kinds of union actions that may be prohibited as "unfair labor practices" in a health care setting.

NLRB v. Massachusetts Nursing Association, 557 F.2d 894 (1st Cir. 1977), is a good example of a case involving an unfair labor practice on the part of a union in the health care field. In this case, the NLRB found against the union, and a federal court of appeals agreed with the board. Specifically, the NLRB found that a nurses' union was guilty of bargaining in bad faith. The nurses' union insisted that an "interest arbitration" clause be added to its hospital contract. Under such a clause, issues in dispute between the hospital and the union would be subject to binding arbitration. According to the NLRB, the union could seek inclusion of an arbitration clause in the contract but could not "insist to impasse" on inclusion of such a clause, because it is not a "mandatory" subject for collective bargaining. "Mandatory" bargaining between employee and employer is limited essentially to wages, hours, and working conditions. A union that insists on bargaining on such nonmandatory subjects as an arbitration clause is guilty of bad faith bargaining.

The court in *Massachusetts Nursing Association* carefully resisted the opportunity to broaden the scope of mandatory bargaining in the health care industry. The union had argued that the unique need to maintain an uninterrupted flow of patient care justified inclusion of interest arbitration clauses among those issues subject to mandatory bargaining. The court, however, pointed out that

Congress had already sought to avoid work stoppages in health care by providing in the Health Care Amendments of 1974 for notice before strikes and picketing and for the use of conciliation machinery. The court was also careful to note that its decision does not prevent health care unions and employers from voluntarily agreeing to an arbitration clause.

Q.11:10 How does enforcement action against unfair labor practices work?

Unfair labor practice charges may be filed by employers, labor unions, or employees. If the General Counsel of the NLRB, acting through regional offices located throughout the country, finds the charges to have merit, he or she will issue a complaint against the employer or union and prosecute the case in a formal hearing before an administrative law judge. The administrative law judge will issue a decision that may be appealed to the board. The board may impose a variety of remedies, including cease and desist orders and, where appropriate, backpay awards.

Q.11:11 To which laboratories does the NLRA apply?

The NLRB does not enforce the NLRA against all clinical laboratories, although, as a practical matter, most laboratories will be subject to it. For hospital laboratories, if the hospital has annual revenues of $250,000 or more and is either proprietary or private nonprofit, hospitals will generally be subject to the Act. The Act will not be applied if the hospital is owned by any unit of federal, state, or local government. For independent laboratories, the NLRA will be applied if a laboratory does $50,000 worth of nonretail business in interstate commerce each year. The NLRB will also enforce the Act if a laboratory does $500,000 worth of retail business each year with substantial purchases and/or sales in interstate commerce. For physicians' office laboratories, the NLRA will be applied if the laboratory is a component of a group practice that has revenues in excess of $250,000 annually.

Q.11:12 Are there any special labor relations provisions affecting health care institutions?

Special provisions of the NLRA, added in 1974, affect strikes and picketing at a health care institution. The special provisions reflect Congress's intent that labor disputes at health care institutions should not be allowed to create an interruption in the delivery of patient care. These provisions generally take the form of extra notice requirements and mandatory mediation by the Federal Mediation and Conciliation Service (FMCS).

The NLRA requires that the union give ten days' notice to the hospital if it intends to engage in a strike, work stoppage, or other concerted refusal to work. In addition, guidelines issued by the NLRB specify that if the union does not commence its strike at the designated time, it must do so within 72 hours, and it must give an additional 12 hours' notice.

Additional notice requirements apply in the event of failed collective bargaining negotiations. During negotiations for the first collective bargaining agreement at a hospital, if the hospital and the union are unable to reach agreement, they must give the FMCS 30 days' notice. During this period, the FMCS will actively try to resolve the dispute, and the parties may neither strike nor lock out. In the case of successive collective bargaining agreements where there is already an agreement in existence, a party wishing to terminate the agreement must give the other party 90 days' notice of its intention. It must also give the FMCS 60 days' notice. Neither side may strike or lock out during these 90- and 60-day periods.

Another aspect of strikes and picketing rules in hospital settings is the so-called ally doctrine. Under the ally doctrine, a strike against a primary employer can be extended to a secondary employer who provides the primary employer with substitute workers during the strike. The NLRB's guidelines take the position that an ally doctrine question that arises out of a labor dispute in the health care industry should be referred to the NLRB's Division of Advice. For a more detailed discussion, see the *Health Care Labor Manual*.

Q.11:13 How have these special health care provisions been applied in actual cases?

The scope of the special health care strikes and picketing provisions, and of the ten-day notice requirement in particular, has been interpreted in several NLRB and federal court cases since these provisions were added to the Act in 1974.

In *District 1199, RWDSU v. First Healthcare Corp.*, 222 NLRB No. 15 (1976), four officers of a nonstriking union engaged in a sympathy strike without giving the ten-day notice required for strikes of health care institutions. The board held that sympathy striking, no less than any other type of striking, falls under the ten-day notice requirement. In fact, the board suggested that the notice requirement must be read broadly to apply to all types of strikes, including recognition strikes, area standard strikes, secondary strikes, and jurisdictional strikes.

In *District 1199-E, National Union of Hospital and Health Care Employees, RWDSU*, 227 NLRB No. 26 (1976), the NLRB ruled that the ten-day notice requirement does not apply to threats to strike or picket, but only to actual strikes and picketing. In *District 1199-E*, 299 NLRB 1010 (1977), the board ruled that ten days' notice was not required when the workers in a nursing home engaged in a certain work stoppage, rather than a strike, to protest the employer's repeated cancellation of grievance meetings.

In *NLRB v. International Brotherhood of Electrical Workers*, 548 F.2d 704 (7th Cir. 1977), *cert. denied*, 434 U.S. 837 (1977), a construction union picketed a hospital as a result of a dispute the union had with an electrical contractor working on a new laboratory building adjacent to the main hospital facility. The court held that Congress intended the ten-day notice provision to apply only to disputes involving a health care institution and its own employees. Therefore, the court held that the construction union could picket without giving the ten-day notice.

In several cases, federal courts have ruled that the ten-day notice requirement does not apply to an individual employee who is not represented by a union. For example, in *Kapiolani Hospital v. NLRB*, 581 F.2d 230 (9th Cir. 1978), an unrepresented employee who had decided to honor a picket line at a hospital had not given her hospital employer ten days' notice of her intended work stoppage. The hospital attempted to fire her, citing, among other reasons, her failure to provide ten days' notice. The court, however, ruled that the ten-day notice requirement applies only to "labor organizations" and not to unrepresented individual employees. [See also *Montefiore Hospital and Medical Center v. NLRB*, 621 F.2d 510 (2d Cir. 1980).]

Q.11:14 What does the Fair Labor Standards Act regulate?

The FLSA, 29 U.S.C. §201 *et seq.*, regulates wages, hours, and child labor conditions. It sets a minimum wage in covered industries and establishes a maximum number of hours to be worked each week without payment of overtime. This statute also prohibits "oppressive child labor" in interstate commerce and has established 16 years as the youngest age for employment in most occupations.

Q.11:15 To which laboratories does the FLSA apply?

The FLSA does not apply to all laboratories. For hospital laboratories, the Act covers employees if the facility is a private non-profit or a proprietary hospital. Hospitals operated by state and local governments, however, may also be subject to the Act. For independent or physicians' office laboratories, the Act covers employees if they are engaged in interstate commerce. Coverage is not automatic but highly likely, especially if a significant portion of the laboratory's purchases or services travel through the stream of interstate commerce.

It should be noted, however, that the Act's provisions cover only "employees." The essence of the employer–employee relationship is the employer's compensation and control of the employee. Thus, the FLSA would not cover a volunteer laboratory worker or an independent contractor. Similarly, employees of an independent contractor working at the laboratory would not be the laboratory's employees, since they are under the control of the independent contractor, not the laboratory.

Q.11:16 What are key requirements of the FLSA?

The FLSA is often described as "placing a floor under wages" and a "ceiling over hours." In other words, the law establishes the minimum wage and sets maximum hours that employees can be required to work before the employer must pay overtime wages. The minimum wage, as of January 1, 1994, was $4.25 per hour. The maximum hours that can be worked in a week before overtime is paid are 40 hours. The FLSA requires equal pay for equal work (see **Q.11:19**, below) and prohibits oppressive child labor.

Q.11:17 What are the major equal employment laws?

The major equal employment laws are the Equal Pay Act of 1963, Title VII of the Civil Rights Act of 1964, the Age Discrimination in Employment Act of 1967, the Rehabilitation Act of 1973, and the Americans with Disabilities Act (ADA) of 1990.

Q.11:18 To what laboratories do the equal employment laws apply?

For hospital laboratories, the Equal Pay Act applies if the FLSA applies (see **Q.11:3**, above). The Equal Pay Act also applies to state and local public hospitals. Title VII applies if the hospital has 15 or more employees for 20 or more weeks during the year. The Age Discrimination in Employment Act applies if the hospital has 20 or more employees for 20 or more weeks during the year. The Rehabilitation Act of 1973 applies if the hospital participates in Medicare or Medicaid. The ADA applies if the hospital has 15 or more employees for each working day in each of 20 or more calendar weeks in the current or preceding calendar year.

For physician's office and independent laboratories, the same criteria apply.

Q.11:19 What does the Equal Pay Act require?

The Equal Pay Act, technically a part of the FLSA, is intended to eliminate sex-based wage differentials by requiring equal pay for equal work. According to the law, "equal work" means jobs "the performance of which requires equal skill, effort, and responsibility, and which are performed under similar working conditions." [See 29 U.S.C. §206(d)(1).] Thus, to be "equal," jobs must pass this four-part test:

1. Equal skill required,
2. Equal effort required,
3. Equal responsibility involved, and
4. Similar working conditions.

Q.11:20 Does the Equal Pay Act mean that jobs have to be identical in order to be "equal"?

Regulatory provisions that implement the law make clear that jobs do not have to be identical in order to be "equal" for purposes of the Equal Pay Act. Rather, the regulations provide that insubstantial differences in the amount of skill, effort, or responsibility required for the job will not render the equal pay standards inapplicable. [29 C.F.R. §800.122] Thus, in evaluating whether jobs are "equal" for purposes of the statute, the employer should look past job titles, classifications, or descriptions to the actual requirements of the jobs themselves.

Q.11:21 Are there any exceptions to the Equal Pay Act?

There are exceptions to the Equal Pay Act. A wage differential is permitted when it is pursuant to a *bona fide* seniority merit system or a system that bases rewards on the quality or quantity of production. [See 29 U.S.C. §206(d)(1).] The system must be rational, consistent, and not involve arbitrary discrimination. An employer will be best protected if the system is formal and written, although a written system is not expressly required. [See 29 C.F.R. §800.144.]

Wage differentials for equal work are also permitted if they are based on some "factor other than sex." The regulations that interpret the Equal Pay Act illustrate what is and is not a "factor other than sex." Granting higher pay to a head of household because of his or her greater responsibilities is forbidden as sex-based, because such a practice tends to favor men over women and is based on considerations that are extraneous to the employee's performance of the job. [See 29 C.F.R. §800.149.] Wage differentials based on perceived differences between the cost of employing men and employing women are also barred as sex-based.

On the other hand, it is permissible to provide unequal pay for equal work to part-time or temporary workers or to permanent workers who are on temporary reassignment. The regulations also explicitly allow an equal pay exemption for a long-service worker who is in ill health. Such an employee may be reassigned to easier work at a lower level while retaining his or her old rate of pay, without compelling a rise in the general wage level in the new position. [See 29 C.F.R. §§100.146–100.151.]

A case illustrating the successful assertion of the "factor other than sex" defense in an Equal Pay Act suit was *EEOC v. Delaware Department of Health & Social Services*, 667 F. Supp. 1057 (D. Del. 1987). In that case, a group of female nurses employed by a public health clinic brought an Equal Pay Act suit, charging that the Act was violated because they were performing the same work as a male physician's assistant but at lower pay. The court overturned a jury verdict in favor of the nurses, finding that the evidence demonstrated overwhelmingly that the pay differential was due to "a factor other than sex," in this case, a "valid classification system," and that all decisions made regarding wage levels for the physician's assistant and the public health nurses were made under that system.

A contrasting case is *Brennan v. South Davis Community Hospital*, 538 F.2d 859 (10th Cir. 1976). In this case, the Tenth Circuit Court of Appeals affirmed the trial court's finding that hospital male orderlies and female aides performed substantially equal jobs for purposes of the Equal Pay Act. The appellate court also affirmed the lower court's finding that the jobs of maids and janitors were substantially equal.

Q.11:22 What does Title VII of the Civil Rights Act require?

Title VII of the Civil Rights Act, 42 U.S.C. §2000(e), commonly known as "Title VII," is the basic equal employment opportunity statute in the United States. It prohibits all forms of employment-related discrimination on the basis of race, color, religion, sex, or national origin.

Q.11:23 What types of activities are addressed by Title VII?

Specifically, Title VII prohibits discrimination in job advertising, hiring, on-the-job treatment, and job termination. Additionally, the statute prohibits employers from depriving employees of any "employment opportunities." This means that all employees who are equally qualified must have equal access to apprenticeship and training opportunities. (Title VII is not intended, however, to compromise the workings of a legitimate, *bona fide* seniority or merit system, or professionally developed ability or competency tests.)

Q.11:24 What employers are covered by Title VII?

Title VII applies to all employers engaged "in an industry affecting commerce" who employ 15 or more persons for 20 or more weeks during the year, whether such employers operate in the private, nonprofit, or public sectors.

Q.11:25 What are some examples of the application of Title VII to race discrimination in health care settings?

Several federal courts have considered charges of on-the-job racial discrimination in health care settings. It is clear from the following cases that the plaintiff-employee does not always win.

In *McGrath v. Permanente Medical Group*, 532 F. Supp. 6 (N.D. Calif. 1979), a medical technologist brought suit against her employer, a hospital. The employee contended that she had been discharged because of race and sex discrimination. She established that she had been discharged shortly after complaining about the hospital's refusal to assign her to culture and mycology rotations and the hospital's refusal to allow her to take accrued educational leave. The hospital, however, was able to establish that it had discharged the technologist because she had taken her educational leave without permission and had not returned when notified that her discharge was imminent. Further, the hospital established that the technologist had been scheduled for the culture and mycology rotations that she requested, but that it had been impossible to assign her to these rotations because of her unauthorized absence. Therefore, the court ruled that the hospital had met its burden of showing a legitimate, nondiscriminatory reason for discharging the employee.

In *Harris v. Group Health Association*, 662 F.2d 869 (D.C. Cir. 1981), a black microbiologist who had been discharged from the position of chief of microbiology within the laboratory department of a health maintenance organizaion (HMO) contended that the firing was the result of racial discrimination. The D.C. Court Circuit upheld a lower court's decision that the employee was discharged for valid nondiscriminatory reasons, and, in addition, assessed attorney's costs and expenses for the appeal against the microbiologist.

In *Doe v. St. Joseph's Hospital of Fort Wayne*, 788 F.2d 411 (7th Cir. 1986), the Seventh Circuit Court of Appeals considered whether the absence of an employer–employee relationship precludes an individual from bringing a claim under Title VII. In Doe, a Korean physician alleged that the hospital unlawfully revoked her staff privileges in violation of Title VII's prohibition against race discrimination.

The hospital argued that Title VII did not apply because the physician was not an employee of the hospital. The court held, however, that an employment relationship is not a prerequisite to a Title VII claim. The court focused on the statutory language, which makes it an unlawful employment practice for an employer to discriminate against "any individual" with respect to "privileges of employment." The court held that although the physician was not a hospital employee, the language of Title VII does not require an employment relationship; rather, Title VII prohibits an employer from discriminating against "any individual." Moreover, because the hospital had the capacity to control the physician's access to prospective patients who are the physician's ultimate employers, the hospital could affect the physician's privileges of employment. Accordingly, the court ruled that the physician should be allowed to proceed with her claim.

In *Lee v. Loyola University of Chicago*, 658 F. Supp. 1 187 (N.D. Ill. 1987), a black male alleged both discrimination in hiring and discrimination in conditions of employment in connection with his job as a physical therapist at the Loyola University Medical Center. With regard to hiring, the plaintiff alleged that he had applied for the physical therapist position several times, beginning in 1978, but was not hired until 1983. During the time when he was rejected for the position, four white persons with less experience and education than he were hired. The court held that these facts were sufficient to state a case for discrimination in hiring, because, to establish such a case, a plaintiff must show that he belongs to a racial minority, that he applied and qualified for an open position, that he was rejected despite his qualifications, and that the position remained open and the employer continued to seek applicants from persons with qualifications similar to those of the plaintiff. Once the plaintiff establishes these elements of the case for discrimination in hiring, the defendant bears the burden of establishing a legitimate, nondiscriminatory reason for rejecting the plaintiff.

With regard to discrimination in conditions of employment, the plaintiff asserted that he was not provided the same training necessary for job advancement that his white coworkers received. The plaintiff also claimed that such treatment was intentional. The court found that he had adequately stated a case for discrimination in conditions of employment, which is satisfied by intentional disparate treatment of minority workers.

Q.11:26 What has the Equal Employment Opportunity Commission (EEOC) said about sex discrimination in the workplace?

It should be noted that the issue of sexual discrimination in employment is more complex and more rapidly changing than that of racial discrimination. The EEOC has set out, at 29 C.F.R. §1604, detailed guidelines for eliminating sex-based employment discrimination. An employer may discriminate on the basis of sex only if the sex of the employee is itself a "*bona fide* occupational qualification" that is "reasonably necessary to the normal operation" of the business. The mere preference of an employer, of coworkers, or of business clients that the employee be male, for example, does not suffice. An employer may make preemployment inquiry into the sex of the applicant, but not for the purpose of deciding whether or not to hire.

Q.11:27 What are some examples of the application of Title VII to sex discrimination in health care employment settings?

A case in a health care setting that illustrates certain limitations of Title VII's applicability is *DeCintio v. Westchester County Medical*, 807 F.2d 304 (2d Cir. 1986). In that case, seven male respiratory therapists employed by a medical center charged that they had been discriminated against on the basis of sex because they had been unfairly disqualified from promotion to the position of assistant chief respiratory therapist by the program administrator of the respiratory therapy department. The program administrator had initiated a requirement that all applicants for the assistant chief position be registered by the National Board of Respiratory Therapists. The male therapists, who were not so registered, claimed that the administrator initiated this registration requirement in order to disqualify them and to enable him to hire for the assistant chief position a woman with whom he was romantically involved. A trial court found that the evidence in the case supported this claim and that the male therapists had therefore suffered sex discrimination.

The court of appeals reversed, finding that the preferential hiring of the woman for the assistant chief job was due to discrimination on the basis of a romantic relationship with the employer, not on the basis of "sex." The court held that the term *sex* in Title VII was not intended by Congress to include "sexual liaisons" and "sexual attractions." Rather, the term *sex* was limited to its "traditional definition" as "gender." The court pointed out that in this case the male employees faced exactly the same predicament as that faced by any woman applicant for the promotion: "no one but [the Administrator's paramour] could be considered for the appointment because of [her] special relationship to the [Administrator]." [807 F.2d at 308] Because the romantic relationship could have operated to the detriment of all applicants for the position other than the "paramour," both male and female, the male therapists could not claim discrimination on the basis of their sex under Title VII.

In a health care case, a U.S. district court has held that a hospital engages in prohibited sex discrimination when it pays female employees a lower wage than male employees who are performing the same job. In this case, *EEOC v. Harper Grace Hospital*, 689 F. Supp. 708 (E.D. Mich. 1988), two Detroit hospitals paid female custodians 11 cents less per hour than male custodians. Two female custodians filed complaints with the EEOC, which sued the hospitals. The EEOC complaint charged that the hospitals divided custodians into two categories, housekeepers and aides, and paid them different wages. Nearly all of the housekeepers, who received the higher wages, were male, and nearly all of the aides were female.

The court found that the job responsibilities of the two classifications were virtually identical, and the only factors differentiating the two were wages and gender. Thus, the pay differential constituted discrimination on the basis of sex. The court rejected the hospital's arguments that the jobs were different enough to justify different wages and that the pay differential between the male and female employees was part of a union contract.

Q.11:28 How does Title VII deal with pregnancy and maternity?

The area of maternity and child-rearing rights and benefits is undergoing particularly rapid change. Special treatment of a pregnant employee, solely on the basis of her pregnancy, has been attacked by Congress. In 1978, Congress amended Title VII by setting limits on how employers may treat pregnant employees. Specifically, Title VII forbids employment discrimination on the basis of pregnancy, childbirth, and related medical conditions and requires that women affected by pregnancy or childbirth be treated the same as other employees for all employment-related purposes, including the receipt of benefits under fringe-benefit programs.

In June 1983, the Supreme Court affirmed a decision of the Fourth Circuit Court of Appeals that by limiting pregnancy benefits that were available to employees' spouses, the employer's health benefits plan discriminated against male employees. [*Newport News Shipbuilding & Dry Dock Co. v. EEOC*, 103 S.Ct. 2662 (1983)] The court specifically rejected the employer's argument that Title VII's prohibition against pregnancy-based discrimination applies only to employees and not to spouses of employees. The court stated that, for all Title VII purposes, discrimination based on pregnancy is, on its face, discrimination on the basis of sex. Further, the court noted, because the sex of the spouse is always the opposite of the sex of the employee, it follows inevitably that discrimination against female spouses in the provision of fringe benefits also constitutes discrimination against male employees.

Q.11:29 What are some examples of health care cases involving discrimination on the basis of pregnancy or maternity?

Examples of health care cases involving sex discrimination on the basis of pregnancy are as follows.

In *Hayes v. Shelby Memorial Hospital*, 732 F.2d 944 (11th Cir. 1984), a federal appellate court ruled that a hospital violated Title VII by firing a pregnant employee. In this case, the employee was an x-ray technician who was fired after she became pregnant. The hospital justified this action as being necessary to protect the pregnant employee's fetus from potentially harmful radiation and to protect the hospital from exposure to liability as a result of potential litigation.

The appellate court ruled against the hospital's contention that nonpregnancy is a *bona fide* occupational qualification for the x-ray technician's job. The hospital had not successfully asserted that the technician's pregnancy would interfere with her ability to perform her duties or that her fear of potential harm to the fetus might adversely affect her job performance. The court also found that the hospital had failed to prove that the employee's fetus would be exposed to an unreasonable amount of radiation.

At least one case, *Zuniga v. Kleberg Court Hospital*, 662 F.2d 986 (5th Cir. 1982), has involved a charge of pregnancy-based discrimination in a diagnostic department of a hospital. The case was brought by an x-ray technician who was dismissed by her hospital employer because she was pregnant. The hospital feared that the employee's exposure to radiation could harm the health of the fetus and could also expose the hospital to potential liability for this harm.

The court accepted the employee's contention that the hospital's alleged business necessity for terminating her was a pretext for sex discrimination. The hospital's concern over the health of the fetus and its fear of potential liability to the child did not justify dismissal since the hospital had failed to use an available less discriminatory means of achieving its business purpose by granting the employee a leave of absence. At the time the employee was forced to resign, the hospital had a formal policy governing leaves of absence. Although the policy applied to all hospital personnel, the hospital administrator specifically excepted the pregnant employee from its coverage because he believed that it would be difficult to find an x-ray technician to replace her temporarily. The court, however, would not accept the difficulty of temporarily replacing the employee as justification for terminating her.

Q.11:30 Does sexual harassment violate Title VII?

Sexual harassment in the workplace has come under increasing attack in recent years as a form of sex-based employment discrimination. The EEOC has taken the position that sexual harassment is a violation of Title VII and has issued guidelines for employers in this area. [See 29 C.F.R. §1604.11.] According to the EEOC, sexual harassment in violation of Title VII occurs when the following criteria are met:

- There are unwelcome sexual advances, requests for sexual favors, and other verbal or physical conduct of a sexual nature; *and*

- Submission to such conduct is made explicitly or implicitly a condition of an individual's employment; *or*
- Submission to or rejection of such conduct is used as the basis for employment decisions affecting the individual; *or*
- Such conduct has the purpose or effect of substantially interfering with an individual's work performance or creating an intimidating, hostile, or offensive working environment.

Significantly, the EEOC imposes substantial responsibility on employers for preventing sexual harassment. The EEOC guidelines make clear that an employer will generally be liable for acts of its agents or supervisory employees that violate the sexual harassment guidelines, even when the employer did not condone such acts or even know about them:

> . . . [A]n employer . . . is responsible for its acts and those of its agents and supervisory employees with respect to sexual harassment regardless of whether the specific acts complained of were authorized or even forbidden by the employer and regardless of whether the employer knew or should have known of their occurrence. [29 C.F.R. §1604.11]

The guidelines go on to advise that "prevention is the best tool for eliminating sexual harassment." [*Id.*]

Q.11:31 What is an example of the application of Title VII to sex discrimination in employment?

In *Bundy v. Jackson*, 641 F.2d 934 (D.C. Cir. 1981), the court was faced with a Title VII action brought by a woman who alleged that she had been sexually harassed on the job, although her resistance to the harassment had not led to loss of job or of any tangible job benefits. The court ruled that the sexual harassment, by itself, poisoned the work environment for the employee. Hence, the "conditions of employment" for the employee, which include the psychological and emotional work environment, were damaged on the basis of sexual discrimination. By creating this "discriminatory environment" in the workplace through on-the-job sexual harassment, the employer violated Title VII.

For a similar conclusion reached by another federal appeals court, see *Henson v. City of Dundee*, 682 F.2d 897 (11th Cir. 1982).

Q.11:32 What are some examples of the application of Title VII to discrimination on the basis of religion or national origin?

Examples of the application of Title VII to discrimination on the basis of religion and national origin are as follows.

A federal district court has ruled that a hospital did not violate Title VII by terminating a nurse who was unable to work her scheduled shift due to her religious beliefs. [See *Murphy v. Edge Memorial Hospital*, 550 F. Supp. 1185 (M.D. Ala. 1982).] In practicing the tenets of her religion, the nurse refused to work Friday evenings through Saturday at sundown. The court found that it was impossible for the hospital to accommodate this aspect of her beliefs without undue hardship. Specifically, the court found that it was impossible for the hospital to accommodate her beliefs without having other nurses assigned to a disproportionate share of weekend duty, a result that would violate the hospital's neutral scheduling system for nurses.

In *Gomez v. Alexian Brothers Hospital of San Jose*, 698 F.2d 1019 (9th Cir. 1983), a federal appellate court decided a case involving a charge of discrimination on the basis of national origin. In this case, a physician of Hispanic ancestry who had proposed to a hospital that his medical group operate the hospital's emergency department, with himself as the emergency department director, sued under Title VII after this proposal was rejected. The federal district court dismissed his suit on the ground that he lacked standing to sue. The lower court ruled that Title VII does not apply to independent contractors such as the medical group, but only to employment relationships. The Ninth Circuit, however, reversed this decision. On the facts in this case, the appellate court found a sufficient employment link between the physician and the hospital to support the physician's standing to sue. It rejected the hospital's argument that it was the medical group itself, and not the physician, that had been injured.

Q.11:33 How has the EEOC addressed discrimination on the basis of religion or national origin?

In 1980, the EEOC issued guidelines on religious discrimination. The guidelines, at 29 C.F.R. §§1605.1–.3, require an employer to choose the available alternative that least disadvantages the employment opportunities of the employee requiring accommodation of his or her religious beliefs. The guidelines suggest that accommodation attempts include a substitute for the employee when necessary, flexible scheduling, lateral transfer, and change of job assignments. However, it should be noted that the guidelines allow an employer to justify its refusal to accommodate an employee's religious beliefs if the employer can establish that the accommodation would cause "undue hardship."

The EEOC has also issued guidelines regarding discrimination on the basis of national origin. [See 29 C.F.R. Part 1606.] These guidelines define national origin discrimination as including, but not limited to, "the denial of equal employment opportunity because of an individual's, or his or her ancestor's, place of origin; or because an individual has the physical, cultural or linguistic characteristics of a national origin group." [29 C.F.R. §1606.1]

The national origin discrimination guidelines deal with such issues as the lawfulness under Title VII of citizenship requirements and "speak-English-only" rules.

Q.11:34 What activities are affected by the Age Discrimination in Employment Act?

The Age Discrimination in Employment Act (ADEA) of 1967, 29 U.S.C. §621 *et seq.*, protects employees aged 40 to 70 from age discrimination by employers. The Act makes it a violation for an employer to do the following:

- Refuse to hire, or to discharge or otherwise discriminate against, any person with regard to compensation, terms or conditions, or privileges of employment because of that person's age;
- Limit, segregate, or classify employees in any way that would deprive or tend to deprive any person of employment opportunities because of that person's age; or
- Reduce wage rates of any employee in order to comply with the Act.

These provisions are very similar to the prohibitions against discrimination on the basis of race and sex in Title VII.

Q.11:35 Are there any exceptions or defenses to the application of the ADEA?

The Act does permit age-based discrimination where age is a *bona fide* occupational qualification that is reasonably necessary to the normal operation of the business. The Act also allows age-based discrimination pursuant to a *bona fide* employee benefit plan, such as a pension or insurance plan, as long as that plan is not a "subterfuge" to evade the purposes of the Act. [See 29 U.S.C. §623(f)(2).]

Where age is a "*bona fide* occupational qualification reasonably necessary to the normal operation of the particular business," age-based discrimination in employment is allowed. With regard to compulsory and early retirement plans, the Act allows age-based discrimination pursuant to a *bona fide* employee benefit plan such as a retirement, pension, or insurance plan "which is not a subterfuge to evade the purposes" of the Act. [See 29 U.S.C. §623(f)(2).] This exception means that employees can be forcibly retired as part of a reasonable and consistent plan of benefit to the employees.

Q.11:36 What are some examples of cases applying the ADEA in health care settings?

Elliott v. Group Medical & Surgical Service, 714 F.2d 556 (5th Cir. 1983), was an ADEA case in which a federal appellate court ruled in favor of the employer. The case was brought by six executives whose average age was 49.5 years. They were fired as part of a corporate reorganization of a health care third-party payment organization and were replaced by executives whose average age was 36.5 years. In essence, the Fifth Circuit ruled that it is not the court's role to second-guess legitimate management decisions. The court recognized that the terminated employees, all over the age of 40, were replaced by younger persons. However, this fact did not establish age-based discrimination on the part of the employer in view of the employer's evidence that each discharge resulted from a corporate reorganization that was designed to increase management efficiency.

The case of *Nobler v. Beth Israel Medical Center,* 702 F. Supp. 1023 (S.D.N.Y. 1988), illustrates the ability of a health care professional to make a case for age discrimination based on statements that might create an inference of intention to discriminate in hiring on the basis of age. In this case, a physician was among six candidates to head a hospital's newly established department of radiation therapy. The selection process was handled by a six-member search committee. The ages of the candidates ranged from 36 to 57 years, and the aggrieved physician, at 53, was the second oldest. Ultimately, the search committee selected the 36-year-old applicant.

On the basis of these facts, the physician brought an age discrimination suit. The hospital sought to have the case concluded on a motion for summary judgment, arguing that it had "legitimate, nondiscriminatory reasons" for selecting the younger candidate. This argument was based on the fact that the selection of the younger man was made by a committee of eminent physicians and hospital administrators that applied defined selection criteria, including the candidates' academic, clinical, and leadership abilities, and, of paramount importance, the perceived ability of the candidate to present an inspiring vision for the future of the new department.

The court denied the hospital's motion for summary judgment on the grounds of several statements made by committee members in describing their approach to the hiring decision. The court noted that committee members stated that the group was looking for "new blood," a "fresh face," a "new outlook," and "the best leadership . . . into the next century." [702 F. Supp. at 1029] These statements, the court noted, could be construed as reflecting a preference for a director chosen from outside the hospital but could also reflect a preference for youth. Thus, the court concluded, the statements could reasonably be viewed as evidence of discriminatory motives on the part of the committee, requiring that the physician be given an opportunity to go forward with his case and have the jury make the ultimate decision as to whether, in fact, discrimination on the basis of age had occurred.

Q.11:37 Which federal agency, if any, administers and enforces the ADEA?

The Act is administered and enforced by the Department of Labor, but aggrieved employees can bring suit on their own.

Q.11:38 Are there any protections against workplace discrimination on the basis of handicap or disability?

Yes. Section 504 of the Rehabilitation Act of 1973, 29 U.S.C. §797, and the Americans with Disabilities Act, 42 U.S.C. §12101 *et seq.*, both proscribe discrimination on the basis of handicap or disability.

Q.11:39 What do the Rehabilitation Act of 1973 and the Americans with Disabilities Act (ADA) do?

Section 504 applies to federal employers or private employers that participate in programs receiving federal assistance. As interpreted by the courts, the Act applies to employers that participate in Medicare or Medicaid. The ADA, however, applies to all employers in the United States, whether public or private sector, that have 15 or more employees for 20 or more weeks during the year.

Both of these laws prohibit discrimination on the basis of disability or handicap in hiring, firing, placement, and benefits, unless the employer can show that there was a substantial business necessity for the discrimination. Generally, the ADA requires employers to furnish disabled employees a "reasonable accommodation" to permit them to perform the duties of their desired jobs notwithstanding their handicap (for example, a sign language interpreter for a deaf person or braille books or manuals for a blind person).

Title III of the ADA also prohibits discrimination in "public accommodations," which include most service providers and most providers of health care services, including laboratories, physicians' offices, and hospitals. Title III requires providers of services to eliminate criteria that screen out disabled persons from being able to enjoy the benefit of the services or being eligible to receive them.

Title III also requires service providers to provide auxiliary aids so that blind or deaf persons can readily appreciate services and to provide "readily achievable" removal of architectural and transportation barriers that would limit the ability of disabled persons to take advantage of the services provided. "Readily achievable" barrier removal means barrier removal that is easy to accomplish and able to be implemented without much difficulty or expense. Examples of such barrier removal would include making curb cuts, widening doors, widening toilet stalls, raising toilet seats, ramping a few steps, installing flashing fire alarms, removing high-pile carpets, installing grab bars, altering door hardware, lowering telephones, adjusting room layouts, widening parking spaces, and installing vehicle hand controls.

Q.11:40 Are there any defenses or limitations to the requirements of the Rehabilitation Act and the ADA?

These antidiscrimination laws do not require employers to provide "reasonable accommodations" to employees, or offer services to persons, when doing so would constitute an "undue hardship" to the employer or constitute a "direct threat" to the health and safety of other employees. An undue hardship is defined to mean a very substantial financial or operational burden. A direct threat is defined to mean a "significant risk" to the health or safety of others.

Q.11:41 Which agency administers the Rehabilitation Act and the ADA?

Generally, the employment discrimination laws are administered by the EEOC.

Q.11:42 How does the ADA address employer-provided insurance?

The ADA says nothing about whether an employer must or should offer health insurance benefits and does not impose any regulatory constraints on the general terms of an insurance plan—for example, the existence of a deductible or its dollar amount, the cost of a health insurance plan to employees, or the types or identities of health care providers that furnish services under the plan—that are not disability specific. However, the ADA does prohibit "disability-based distinctions" in insurance plans unless the plan meets certain requirements stated in Sections 501(c)(1), (2), and (3) of the Act. Specifically, the plan must be *bona fide*; based on or not inconsistent with state law; and not a subterfuge to evade the purposes of the Act. Under interpretive guidelines established by the EEOC, the employer bears the burden of proof to show that these conditions are satisfied by the particular plan.

Under the EEOC guidelines, a plan will be treated as *bona fide* if it exists and pays benefits, and its terms have been accurately communicated to employees who are eligible to participate in the plan. As to a basis in or consistency with state law, the EEOC guidelines provide that the determination of compliance with state law will be based on the interpretation of that law by the appropriate state authorities. As to subterfuges to evade the purposes of the Act, the EEOC guidelines define a "subterfuge" as a disability-based disparate treatment that is not justified by risks or costs.

Q.11:43 What are the major laws affecting occupational safety and health?

The major laws affecting occupational safety and health are the federal Occupational Safety and Health Act (OSHA Act), 29

U.S.C. §651 *et seq.*, and laws in certain states, such as California, that are similar in purpose and effect.

Q.11:44 Which agency enforces the occupational safety and health laws?

The federal OSHA Act is administered by the Occupational Safety and Health Administration (OSHA) within the Department of Labor. State laws similar to the federal OSHA Act are administered by similar agencies at the state level.

Q.11:45 How does the OSHA Act affect clinical laboratory activities?

The purpose of the OSHA Act is to establish legal requirements relating to the safety of the employee working environment. Under the so-called general duty clause of the Act, every covered employer has the general duty to furnish each of his or her employees an employment environment and conditions that are free from recognized hazards that may cause death or serious physical harm.

The Act applies to every employer "engaged in a business affecting commerce" [29 U.S.C. §652(5)], a phrase reflecting Congress' intent to reach to the fullest extent of congressional regulatory powers over business in the United States. In practical terms, the OSHA Act applies to nearly all employers except federal, state, or municipal government. Thus, the Act applies to virtually all clinical laboratories in the private sector. This means that laboratories must comply with specific regulations of the Occupational Safety and Health Administration concerning occupational safety and health.

Q.11:46 What are the "bloodborne pathogens" regulations?

The bloodborne pathogens regulations, 29 C.F.R. §1910.1030 *et seq.*, comprise one of the most important aspects of the OSHA regulations that affect clinical laboratories. The purpose of these regulations is to eliminate or minimize occupational exposure to hepatitis B virus (HBV), human immunodeficiency virus (HIV), and other bloodborne pathogens. The regulations reflect OSHA's determination that health care workers are at significant risk for exposure to these pathogens when they come into contact with blood and other potentially infectious materials and that a variety of work practices and equipment can significantly reduce such exposure.

Q.11:47 What are some of the actions a laboratory must take to comply with the bloodborne pathogens regulations?

Generally, the regulations require employers to develop and implement a written Exposure Control Plan to minimize the risk of occupational exposure to blood and infectious materials. The plan must provide for implementation of certain standards contained in the regulations, including the Centers for Disease Control and Prevention's "universal precautions;" engineering and work practice controls; and the use of personal protective equipment, such as gloves, gowns, and masks. The regulations contain specific standards for disposal of sharps and other contaminated waste and require that employers provide HBV vaccinations to all employees who have occupational exposure. The regulations require certain labeling standards for containers of infectious waste and mandate that employers must provide all employees who have occupational exposure to bloodborne pathogens with a training program concerning the requirements of the regulations. Additionally, the regulations specify recordkeeping standards, including requirements for medical records for employees who have incidents of occupational exposure.

These regulations are lengthy and complex. For a more extensive summary of their requirements, see L.R.M., Part 10.2, Section 6-2.

12

Malpractice

Q.12:1 What is malpractice?

Malpractice is, in legal terms, negligence. Negligence is the failure to render the care that is due to the patient under the circumstances when such failure proximately and foreseeably results in harm to the patient.

The concept of malpractice may be illustrated by the questions that a court would probably ask in any lawsuit against a laboratory for malpractice:

- What professional standards of care should the laboratory have followed in this case?
- Did the laboratory fail to meet this standard of care?
- Was it foreseeable that the patient would be harmed as a result of the laboratory's failure to meet the professional standard of care?
- Was the patient's injury proximately caused by the laboratory's failure to meet this professional standard of care?

It should be noted that the law of malpractice does not require laboratories to be completely free of mistakes. As one administrative law judge has commented, "No laboratory, regardless of the quality of its personnel, equipment, procedures and techniques, will ever be mistake-free, and . . . [no] . . . flawless pathology laboratory exists. It is a goal to strive for, but it is probably beyond the grasp of mere mortals." [*In the Matter of United Medical Laboratories,*

Inc., Social Security Administration, Bureau of Hearings and Appeals, Docket No. PF-62 (1974) at 33] While this comment was not made in the context of a malpractice suit, the judge's observation does reflect a general understanding that no laboratory can avoid making some mistakes. Rather, in order to be guilty of malpractice, the laboratory must make a mistake that reflects a failure to follow generally accepted professional laboratory standards.

Q.12:2 What is an example of a laboratory malpractice case?

A good example of how a laboratory can incur malpractice liability and the consequences is the case of *Schnebly v. Baker,* 217 N.W.2d 708 (Iowa 1974). In that case, an infant shortly after its birth, manifested clinical symptoms that suggested the possibility of imminent brain damage. Tests performed at the local hospital indicated that the child's bilirubin level was rising dangerously. The child's family physician took the child to a pediatrician on the staff of a large hospital in another city. The pediatrician ignored the symptoms and the laboratory test results from the first hospital, and instead relied solely on tests performed by the laboratory in his own hospital. These tests, in contrast to the earlier ones, revealed a low level of bilirubin. The laboratory in the second hospital did not have a regular procedure for ensuring that the reagents it used were reliable and could be counted on to produce accurate results. In fact, the reagent this laboratory used to test the child's bilirubin level was overaged, had deteriorated, and consequently yielded incorrect results. The tests at the first hospital had been correct: the child's bilirubin level was increasing dangerously, and as a result, the child suffered grave and permanent brain damage. This condition, as the trial court later noted, was "catastrophic," but could have been avoided by prompt treatment if the second laboratory's tests had correctly identified the child's rising bilirubin level. The parents sued on behalf of the child and to recover damages for their own mental suffering caused by the damage to him.

In this case, several parties could have been viewed as negligent: the second hospital laboratory (and the two pathologists who ran it) for failing to ensure the reliability of its reagents; the pediatrician who relied exclusively on the test results from this laboratory and ignored contradictory clinical symptoms and earlier test results; and the hospital itself on the theory that the facility is responsible for errors of its operating units and physician staff. In fact, the court imposed liability on all parties, the pediatrician, the pathologist who ran the hospital laboratory, and the hospital itself for the errors of these persons. Together, these parties sustained a damage award of over $900,000 (an amount that equals millions in 1994 dollars).

The *Schnebly* case is notable for the amount of attention the court devoted to the liability of the laboratory and the court's refusal to find that liability superseded by the error of the pediatrician. In considering the liability of the laboratory and the pathologist who ran it, the court focused on the "critical nature" of the laboratory's services: "[The laboratory's] function constituted a vital part of the diagnostic and therapeutic process on which a child's life depended. The laboratory played a major role in the process, tending to increasing its responsibility for the ultimate result." [217 N.W.2d at 730]

The court also emphasized the pervasive nature of the laboratory's negligence:

> This was not an isolated fluke in a single test. The reagent had deteriorated over a period of time. For this patient alone, the laboratory ran not one but several faulty tests. The test results were not merely erroneous to a degree; they were completely wrong. The extent of the laboratory's culpability tends to extend the causal effect of its negligence. [217 N.W.2d at 730]

Although a laboratory's negligence will not always produce or contribute to the devastating results experienced by the child in the *Schnebly* case, the court's statements in that case concerning the critical role the laboratory plays in the diagnostic process are applicable to a variety of scenarios and help to explain the basis for potential malpractice liability when a laboratory makes mistakes in the testing process.

Q.12:3 What aspects of the laboratory testing process can give rise to allegations of malpractice?

Numerous aspects of the laboratory testing process can give rise to allegations of malpractice. A few examples are as follows. Malpractice allegations can arise from errors in the following:

- The interpretation of physician test orders;
- The collection and recording of samples;
- The testing process itself, including the activities of testing personnel and the calibration and maintenance of equipment and supplies;
- The reporting of test results; and
- Refusal or failure to perform the test a physician has ordered.

Q.12:4 What is an example of a case involving negligence in collecting or handling samples?

An example of a case involving negligence in specimen collection is *Morrison v. MacNamara*, discussed in the answer to **Q.12:9**, below.

A case involving negligence in the handling of samples is *Parker v. Port Huron Hospital*, 361 Mich. 1, 105 N.W.2d 1 (1960). In that case, a woman entered a hospital for a routine hysterectomy. A technician at the hospital laboratory collected a blood sample from the woman and then confused it with other patient samples. As a result of the confusion, the laboratory recorded an incorrect blood type for the patient. During the hysterectomy procedure, she received a transfusion of blood that was mismatched because her blood type had been recorded incorrectly. As a direct result of the mismatched transfusion, she died a lingering and painful death from kidney failure. Subsequently, her husband sued and recovered damages from the hospital for the suffering and death that the hospital laboratory's negligence had caused his wife.

Q.12:5 What is an example of a case involving laboratory liability for malpractice in the testing process?

A case illustrating a laboratory's malpractice liability for errors in testing is *Gallager v. Duke University*, 852 F.2d 773 (4th Cir. 1988). In that case, parents had a chromosome analysis done on their older child by a hospital laboratory and a cytogeneticist who worked there. The laboratory and the cytogeneticist concluded on the basis of their tests that the child had no genetic abnormalities. Relying on this conclusion, the parents proceeded to conceive a second child, who was born with severe physical and mental abnormalities. Subsequent tests on the second child and the father revealed a genetic abnormality. The parents sued the hospital laboratory and the cytogeneticist, arguing that if the genetic abnormality had been identified in the tests they performed on the couple's first child, they would have decided not to conceive a second child. The parents sued for "wrongful life," seeking to recover damages for the expenses of caring for the severely damaged second child and for the emotional distress they suffered themselves.

The defendants, the hospital and the cytogeneticist, argued that a claim for "wrongful life" could not be recognized by the courts of North Carolina, but the court disagreed. The court held that North Carolina does recognize claims for "wrongful life" due to medical malpractice and that the hospital laboratory and the cytogeneticist had departed from acceptable levels of care when they erroneously tested the couple's first child. Since the parents relied on this incorrect analysis, the court reasoned, the negligence of the hospital laboratory was the proximate, or immediate, cause of the birth of the seriously damaged second child. The court of appeals also held that the parents could seek recovery for their emotional distress because such distress was a foreseeable result of giving birth to and caring for a severely handicapped child.

Q.12:6 What is an example of a case involving laboratory malpractice liability for malpractice based on errors in the calibration and maintenance of equipment and supplies?

An example of such a case is *Schnebly v. Baker*, discussed in the answer to **Q.12:2**, above.

Q.12:7 What is an example of a case involving laboratory malpractice liability for errors in reporting test results?

A case illustrating laboratory malpractice liability for errors in reporting test results is *Waits v. United States*, 611 F.2d 550 (5th Cir. 1980). In that case, a culture and sensitivity (C&S) was ordered for the plaintiff on December 26, 1972, but the results were not made available to his physician by the hospital laboratory or placed on the patient's chart until more than ten days later. By this time, the patient, who had been admitted to the hospital for a compound fracture of the right hip, had been discharged. During the patient's hospital stay, an infection in the area of the fractures appeared, and he was treated with Keflex, an antibiotic. The C&S test was ordered to provide information about that infection and its response to treatment with Keflex. After the patient's discharge, he was transferred to a second hospital, which performed a second C&S test on January 6, 1973. The results of this test showed a deep bone infection that was resistant to Keflex. Although antibiotics existed that could have treated the infection, none had been prescribed for the plaintiff in the first hospital because no information had indicated that his infection was resistant to the Keflex that he had taken. By the time the second C&S test showed this resistance, the bone infection had become so severe that amputation was necessary.

The plaintiff sued the first hospital, arguing that, had the results of its C&S test been made available promptly (according to local standards, which required providing results of C&S tests to ordering physicians within 72 hours), the treating physicians would have known of the infection's resistance to Keflex, prescribed an effective antibiotic, and thus avoided the need to amputate the patient's leg. Ultimately, the patient recovered damages against the hospital laboratory for its negligence in reporting his test results promptly to the treating physicians.

Q.12:8 What is an example of laboratory malpractice liability for failure to perform ordered tests?

A case illustrating a laboratory's malpractice liability for failure to perform tests ordered by a physician is *Monroe Doss v. United*

States, No. 78-488 C(2) (E.D. Mich. 1979). In that case, the patient went to a veterans' hospital for a swollen foot. At several points during his hospital stay, his treating physician ordered tests, but the hospital laboratory did not perform them. As a result of this error, among others, the plaintiff's condition deteriorated so seriously that he had to have a below-the-knee amputation. Ultimately, the veterans' hospital was found to have been negligent in failing to perform the tests that had been ordered.

Q.12:9 What is the standard of care that a clinical laboratory must meet?

The laboratory is held to a standard of care that compares its performance with the performance of other similarly situated laboratories. In some jurisdictions, this comparison is limited to other laboratories situated in the same community or locality. This doctrine is generally called the "locality rule." An increasing number of jurisdictions have rejected the locality rule in favor of a national standard. In either case, the court will consider what specific aspects of laboratory practice and performance are called for under the applicable local or national standard of care.

The following cases illustrate the difference between a local and national standard of care, and the considerations that go into the determination of whether a local or national standard applies.

In *Morrison v. MacNamara*, 407 A.2d 555 (D.C. Cir. 1979), the issues involved procedures for obtaining specimens. A technician-employee of the defendant laboratory attempted to draw a specimen for a urethral smear test while the patient was standing up. This was the procedure commonly followed in the District of Columbia metropolitan area. The patient complained of feeling faint. The technician stopped the sample collection procedure. Several minutes later, he asked the patient whether the procedure could be continued, and the patient said yes. During the sample collection procedure, the patient fainted and struck his head, incurring injury. The patient then sued both the technician and the laboratory for malpractice, alleging that the laboratory should have met the national standard of care, which called for the collection of the specimen while the patient was sitting or lying down. At trial, the plaintiff-patient presented expert testimony concerning the national standard of care for collection of a specimen for the type of test involved. However, the judge instructed the jury to disregard that testimony and to consider only whether the laboratory technician had followed the local standard of care adequately. The Court of Appeals reversed, holding that the laboratory should meet the national standard of care, rather than the local standard. The Court of Appeals reached this conclusion because the laboratory was nationally certified, located in the nation's capital, and operated in a medically sophisticated metropolitan area.

In *Grimes v. Green*, 746 P.2d 978 (Idaho 1987), the issues involved a physician's failure to order certain prenatal tests. The plaintiff was a pregnant woman who, shortly before her due date, experienced weakness, nausea, and pain. She was given a blood test that identified a bacterial infection. However, the hospital's obstetrician/gynecologist who attended her failed to order an amniocentesis to detect amnionitis, a bacterial infection of the amniotic fluid surrounding the fetus. Ultimately, this bacterial infection became life-threatening to the woman, and a hysterectomy became necessary to save her life.

As a result, the plaintiff sued. Experts testifying on her behalf stated that a national standard of care existed for board-certified obstetricians/gynecologists, and that the hospital's obstetrician/gynecologist had violated that standard of care through his failure to order an amniocentesis to diagnose amnionitis. An expert testifying for the physician, on the other hand, testified that amniocentesis was not routinely practiced in the locality because of the concern that the insertion of a needle into the amniotic sac might convey the bacteria from other tissue into the sac. The trial court accepted the patient's contention that a national standard should prevail, but the Court of Appeals reversed, based on a state statutory provision that required use of a "community" standard of care in malpractice cases.

Q.12:10 Can a laboratory be liable for acts of its personnel?

In theory, every person involved in the laboratory testing procedure may be held liable for that individual's own negligence. For example, if a patient is harmed because the laboratory technologist is careless in performing a test, that technologist could be sued. In practice, however, the patient probably would sue the laboratory rather than the technologist, simply because the laboratory is more likely to have the resources, through insurance or otherwise, to pay the damages the plaintiff would win in a lawsuit. Generally, the laboratory will be liable if it is the employer of the person whose error caused harm to the plaintiff, under the principle of "*respondeat superior*," which holds an employer responsible for the conduct of its employees when they are acting in the course of their employment.

Questions of laboratory liability for personnel actions usually involve determining whether such personnel are employees as opposed to independent contractors. Courts usually find that an employment relationship exists when the employer compensates the employee and, to some degree, controls the employee's actions. In the case of laboratory technicians and medical technologists, personnel are likely to be deemed employees for whose acts the laboratory is liable, because these workers are typically paid wages and move from task to task at the discretion and direction of laboratory management. However, a pathologist may not be considered an employee of a laboratory. If a pathologist contracts with the laboratory to provide services as a consultant rather than as an employee, and if that individual retains and uses independent judgment that is his or hers by right as a physician, a court may find the pathologist to be an independent contractor rather than an employee of the laboratory. If so, the laboratory might not be liable for that pathologist's errors.

Q.12:11 What is an example of laboratory liability for acts of personnel?

A case illustrating the liability of a clinical laboratory for a technician's improper test performance is *Pines v. Dr. Carlos D. Moreno, Inc.*, 569 So. 2d 203 (La. App. 1st Cir. 1990). In that case, the mother of an infant born with an unpreventable congenital defect called Cornelia de Lange's syndrome brought suit on behalf of herself and the child against a clinic that included a testing laboratory. The plaintiff had visited the clinic for a suspected pregnancy and had been examined by nurses and a physician. She alleged that during the visit, she submitted a urine sample for testing by the clinic's laboratory, and the test was performed negligently by a laboratory technician. The woman alleged that the improper performance of the test caused the result to read negative when in fact she was pregnant, and caused the physician who examined her to say that she was not pregnant and to prescribe birth control pills for her. The birth control pills aggravated the congenital defect with which the child she was carrying eventually was born. The plaintiff alleged that, if the pregnancy test had been performed correctly, her pregnancy would have been identified, and she would have received proper prenatal care, which would have precluded the prescribing of birth control pills and thus avoided aggravating the child's defect.

Even though the defect was unpreventable, the appellate court that decided the case held that, because the incorrect performance of the test only resulted in aggravating the condition, the defendant clinic could be liable for the negligent test performance of the technician in its laboratory. The court noted that the duty to diagnose a pregnancy correctly encompasses "foreseeable risk that the unborn child will be affected by improper prenatal care." [569 So. 2d at 209]

Q.12:12 Can a laboratory be liable for failure to disclose information?

Yes. Generally, a laboratory will be held to a duty to report test results to the person who ordered the test and to ensure that information relevant to a patient's health is communicated to the person who ordered the test. The extent of this duty appears to be broadening and rests on the premise that an obligation exists to disclose all relevant information to a patient to enable that individual to make an informed decision about future treatment. Generally, the duty falls on the physician, but it can be triggered by the laboratory testing process as well.

Q.12:13 Can a laboratory be liable for disclosure of confidential information?

Yes. In some situations, the disclosure of medical information about a patient can result in harm to that patient. The context in which such disclosure most often causes harm is that of an HIV-positive patient, whose HIV-positive status may result in employment discrimination, including job loss or job transfer, loss of health insurance, or social ostracism. Particularly in those states that have enacted statutes placing severe restrictions on the disclosure of HIV-testing results, a laboratory's disclosure of such information to persons who are not authorized to receive it may subject the laboratory to a lawsuit for statutory negligence. (Usually those authorized by statute to receive the results of HIV testing are limited to the test subject and his or her physician.)

Q.12:14 What is the standard of care to which a physician using laboratory services will be held?

Physicians face the possibility of malpractice liability in their interactions with clinical laboratories if they fail to meet the "ordinary physician" standard. This standard holds that a physician owes a patient the duty to provide that level of care that would be furnished by a physician of ordinary skill and knowledge under the same or similar circumstances. This standard translates into the question: What would have been done had the "ordinary physician" stood in the shoes of the physician who is accused of malpractice?

If the "ordinary physician" would have rejected, as professionally inadequate, the course of action that the defendant-physician followed, the defendant may have committed malpractice. On the other hand, if the "ordinary physician" would have accepted as professionally sufficient the course of action the defendant-physician actually followed, the defendant probably has met the "ordinary physician" standard and is unlikely to be held liable. Courts consider the expert testimony of other physicians to establish the specific practices that the "ordinary physician" standard requires under the specific circumstances of any particular case. Since no two cases are identical, the "ordinary physician" standard varies from case to case. As with a laboratory, a national or local standard may apply, depending on the law of the particular state where the lawsuit occurs.

It should be noted, again, that malpractice is not the same thing as making a mistake, particularly in the context of medical practice, where physicians must make judgments in which honest differences of opinion exist. An ordinarily competent physician who orders all the normally indicated tests but selects the wrong diagnosis from several reasonable possibilities will not generally be held liable for malpractice. The law places greater emphasis on the thoroughness with which the physician approaches a medical question than on the correctness of the solution he or she she chooses.

The following case illustrates the application of the "ordinary physician" standard. In *Groeger v. Colles Orthopedic Assoc.*, 540 N.Y.S.2d 109 (App. Div. 1989), a physician had examined pathology slides to determine whether a tumor was benign or malignant. He failed to make a correct diagnosis, but a medical expert testified that the pathologic examination the physician performed was within accepted standards for ordinary physicians and that the physician's inability to make a correct diagnosis did not constitute a deviation from accepted medical practice. A judgment for the physician was affirmed.

Q.12:15 What acts or omissions by a physician could give rise to allegations of malpractice?

Allegations of physician malpractice can result from the following:

- Failure to order needed tests,
- Failure to detect incorrect test results,
- Misdiagnosis of correct test results,
- Failure to review test results,
- Failure to report test results to the patient,

- Failure to inform a patient of the existence of tests that may shed light on a suspected diagnosis, or
- Failure to warn the patient about the risks of refusing tests that the physician considers necessary.

Q.12:16 What are some examples of physician malpractice in connection with laboratory testing?

Some examples of malpractice liability for physicians using laboratory tests are as follows.

Physicians' failure to order needed tests was at issue in *McNeill v. United States*, 519 F. Supp. 283 (D.S.C. 1981). There, the court found that physicians in the emergency department of an Air Force hospital deviated from the applicable standard of care when they failed twice to examine properly, order laboratory tests for, and prescribe aggressive antibiotic treatment of a ten-month-old child with fever, a swollen and discolored hand, and a rash. Eventually, the child developed a severe case of meningitis that left him crippled and damaged. The court found the United States, the employer of the physicians, liable for their negligence in failing to order the necessary tests to identify the child's condition and treat it properly.

Physician misdiagnosis of correct laboratory test results was involved in *Atkins v. Strayhorn*, 223 Calif. at 3d 1380, 273 Calif. Rptr. 231 (Calif. App. 1990). The test involved was a simple blood count. The plaintiff was a 69-year-old man who appeared at a hospital emergency department complaining of shaking, paleness, and nausea. The man had a history of diabetes. The emergency department physician examined the man and ordered several tests, including a blood count, cultures, electrocardiogram, and others. The emergency department physician found no source of infection to explain the patient's symptoms and requested a consultation with the defendant, who was an internist on call that night. Even though the blood-count test results showed an elevated white blood cell count, possibly indicating a bacterial infection, the internist diagnosed the patient as having a viral infection and did not prescribe antibiotics. He sent the patient home and scheduled a follow-up visit. By the next day, the plaintiff's condition had deteriorated, and finally x-rays revealed a piece of glass in his foot, and another blood culture test revealed a bacterial infection. By this time, however, the plaintiff's condition had worsened so much that antibiotics could not conquer the infection. Consequently, gangrene developed, requiring a partial amputation of the patient's leg. The patient sued the internist for negligence because of the physician's failure to interpret the blood-count test correctly as indicating a bacterial infection. The internist was found negligent by a trial court, and an appeals court affirmed his liability.

A physician's failure to report test results was at issue in the case of *Robak v. United States*, 658 F.2d 471 (7th Cir. 1981). In that case, the plaintiff developed a rash and fever when she was about one month pregnant. Her doctor at an Army medical clinic told her that an initial test for rubella was negative. The plaintiff received a second rubella test a few days later, but the physician never told her that its result was positive, even though she visited the clinic regularly during her pregnancy. The plaintiff's daughter was born with hearing loss, bilateral cataracts, a heart defect, and possible mental retardation—all common symptoms of a rubella syndrome child. She sued the government as the employer of the physician for his failure to inform her of the results of the second rubella test. The Court of Appeals, affirming the government's liability for the actions of the physician, ruled that the physician at the clinic deprived the plaintiff of the opportunity to make an informed decision about whether to have an abortion when he failed to tell her about the positive rubella test and potential consequences of rubella to the fetus she was carrying.

For other examples of physician malpractice liability related to the use of clinical laboratory tests, see L.R.M., Part 12.1, Section 7.

Q.12:17 Are there statutes of limitations that apply to laboratory malpractice?

Yes. If a laboratory commits malpractice and the patient neglects to bring a lawsuit, the patient ultimately will be barred from recovery by the state statute of limitations. Statutes of limitations exist in every state in order to prevent courts from being cluttered indefinitely with old lawsuits and to protect potential defendants from being sued many years after the alleged injury, at a time when it would be difficult to defend against the plaintiff's claims. The applicable statute sets a cut-off date after an injury, beyond which an action to recover from the injury may not be brought. The cut-off point typically is two or three years after the injury occurs.

In some states, the time period begins to run at the point when the injury is discovered by the plaintiff, rather than when the injury actually occurs. For example, in *Peterson v. St. Cloud Hosp.*, 460 N.W.2d 635 (Minn. Ct. App. 1990), the patient sued a pathologist who allegedly had misdiagnosed the patient's cancer. The pathologist had interpreted a slide containing cells of a tumor biopsied from the patient's lung. The pathologist's report indicated that the tumor cells were "suggestive" of a small-cell carcinoma. Chemotherapy and radiation were administered, but the patient did not respond. After a second biopsy, the pathologist identified the patient's problem as a bronchial carcinoid tumor, a condition that would not be improved by chemotherapy or radiation, but rather should be addressed either by surgery or simple close monitoring for the possibility of growth. The plaintiff's subsequent lawsuit alleged that, due to the misdiagnosis of the cancer based on the first biopsy, the plaintiff sustained serious injuries, including those caused by painful and debilitating chemotherapy and radiation treatment that was not appropriate for her actual condition. The defendants argued, among other things, that a two-year statute of limitations barred the action. The trial court agreed, holding that the statute began to run at the time of the pathologist's misdiagnosis of small-cell carcinoma. However, the Court of Appeals reversed, holding that the cause of action did not accrue until the plaintiff suffered damage due to the alleged negligence, and that damage did not occur until the plaintiff discovered her injury as a result of the painful and debilitating chemotherapy and radiation treatments—an event that occurred within the statute of limitations.

Q.12:18 How, if at all, have the states acted to reform the malpractice system in recent years?

In response to growing numbers of malpractice lawsuits and multimillion-dollar recoveries that result in substantial increases in malpractice insurance premiums, some state legislatures have pursued solutions to a perceived "medical malpractice crisis." These statutory solutions generally limit the amount that a successful plaintiff can collect for malpractice; establish administrative mechanisms, such as arbitration and pretrial screening, to handle malpractice actions in lieu of lawsuits; or require a potential plaintiff to give a health care provider notice of his or her intent to sue within a prescribed time period prior to filing suit.

Some such laws have been challenged on constitutional grounds, with varying results. For example, in *Pearlstein v. Maluney,* 500 So. 2d 585 (Fla. Dist. Ct. App. 1986), the plaintiff brought a constitutional challenge to Florida's malpractice reform statute, arguing that the statutory requirement that a prospective plaintiff serve upon each prospective defendant a notice of intent to initiate litigation before commencing suit was unconstitutional. The plaintiff argued that this statutory provision constituted unreasonable discrimination against medical malpractice litigants, thus depriving them of the constitutional right of access to the courts. The plaintiff also challenged the statutory provision as unconstitutionally vague. The trial court agreed, but the Court of Appeals reversed. As to the access to the courts and discrimination arguments, the Court of Appeals pointed out that reasonable restrictions may be placed on the right of access to the courts when such restrictions are in the public interest. The court found that the mere delay of formal medical malpractice litigation through the requirement of prior notice does not constitute a deprivation of access to the courts. As to the claim of vagueness, the court rejected the argument that the statute was unclear merely because it failed to specify any particular form for the prelitigation notice beyond the requirement that the notice be in writing.

A state malpractice statute's damage limitation provision was challenged in the case of *Sibly v. Board of Supervisors of Louisiana State University,* 477 So.2d 1094 (La. 1985). The Louisiana State malpractice damage limitation at issue was $500,000. The plaintiff in the case was a 19-year-old woman who suffered serious and permanent mental and physical injuries due to the malpractice of a hospital that was run by the Louisiana State University Board of Supervisors. Although the plaintiff proved that the hospital's malpractice was the cause of her injuries and that her damages would greatly exceed the statutory limit, the lower courts applied the limitation. The plaintiff argued that the limitation did not apply to the negligence of the University Board of Supervisors (as opposed to the negligence of the hospital) in permitting the medical center's treatment method, which involved psychiatric treatment and administration of drugs by teams without independent peer review. The court agreed with the plaintiff, interpreting the malpractice statute as applying only to actions of malpractice by health care professionals, and not to the independent liability of the hospital's governing board in setting policy. This case illustrates that, despite restrictions imposed by state malpractice statutes, it may still be possible for plaintiffs who suffer extremely severe injuries to obtain full compensation for those injuries.

Q.12:19 Are there any federal laws related to malpractice by health care professionals?

Yes. During the late 1980s, Congress decided to make use of malpractice-related information in collecting and disseminating data about the professional competence and conduct of physicians and other health care practitioners. In the Health Care Quality Improvement Act of 1986, P.L. 99-660, Congress authorized the Secretary of the Department of Health and Human Services (HHS) to establish a computer data bank called the National Practitioner Data Bank to collect and disseminate certain data about the professional conduct of physicians and other practitioners.

HHS has issued regulations implementing this law. These regulations, 45 C.F.R. Part 60, require certain organizations and individuals to report to the data bank certain information about physicians' and other practitioners' professional conduct and competence. Among those who are required to report such information are individuals and entities, including insurance companies, that make payments as a result of medical malpractice actions or claims. The regulations also establish procedures that permit individuals or entities to retrieve information from the data bank or to dispute the accuracy of information about them. Additionally, the regulations require certain entities, such as hospitals that are hiring staff physicians, to consult the bank in certain situations.

The establishment of the bank means that malpractice lawsuits filed against physicians regarding their use of clinical laboratory tests may now have broader impact than immediate financial liability for the alleged malpractice.

Index

Note: Numbers indicate chapter and question numbers not page numbers (e.g., 1:3 indicates Chapter 1, question 3)

N

O

P

R

S

T

U

W

About the Author

Christina Fleps, JD, a partner in the Washington, D.C., law firm of O'Connor & Hannan, handles legislative, regulatory, and litigation matters with concentration in the health care field. Ms. Fleps holds a Juris Doctor degree from the University of California at Berkeley, a Masters of Business Administration from the George Washington University, and a B.A. from Pomona College. Issues addressed in her work include federal and state quality regulation of health care services; federal and state fraud and abuse provisions; Medicare and Medicaid reimbursement for a variety of medical goods and service providers; federal mortgage insurance for hospitals and nursing homes; tax-exempt bond authority for hospitals; and laws and regulations affecting drug testing, AIDS, health care employment discrimination, and FDA regulation of medical devices.

Ms. Fleps has served as an officer of Women In Government Relations and is currently a member of the President's Club of the Women's Legal Defense Fund. She serves on the Technical Advisory Committee of the National Health Policy Council, a nonprofit bipartisan health reform education organization. She speaks and writes widely on a variety of health care issues. Among her publications and addresses are: "Medicare: You Can't Stop Thinking about Tomorrow," "Medicare: Past, Present and Future," "AIDS and the Laboratory," "The ADA and the Laboratory," "Health Reform Update," *The Ophthalmic Reimbursement Manual*, and numerous others.